# Praise for the First Edition of
## *Building a Bridge*

"A welcome and much-needed book that will help bishops, priests, pastoral associates, and all church leaders more compassionately minister to the LGBT community. It will also help LGBT Catholics feel more at home in what is, after all, their church."

—Cardinal Kevin Farrell, Prefect of the Vatican's Dicastery for Laity, Family, and Life

"The Gospel demands that LGBT Catholics must be genuinely loved and treasured in the life of the church. They are not. In *Building a Bridge,* James Martin provides us with the language, perspective, and sense of urgency to undertake the arduous but monumentally Christlike task of replacing a culture of alienation with a culture of encounter and merciful inclusion."

—Robert W. McElroy, Bishop of San Diego

"The Catholic community should thank Father James Martin for writing *Building a Bridge.* Many lesbian, gay, bisexual, and transgender Catholics have spent years on the margins of our community inviting such dialogue. This book cracks open a new door to opportunities to ask important questions about the inclusion of LGBT Catholics in the church, and those opportunities should be seized."

—Editorial, *National Catholic Reporter*

"An admirable call for a courteous conversation that needs to grow. . . . Martin's book is also a helpful spiritual resource. He devotes the second half to 'Biblical Passages for Reflection and Meditation' and concludes with a moving 'A Prayer for When I Feel Rejected.' The biblical texts and Martin's questions for reflection will help LGBT Catholics as well as their families and friends explore their relationship with God in the face of their struggles and in the light of their dignity grounded in God's love. James Martin's message is a 'no-brainer.' But Catholics still need to hear it publicly."

—*The Tablet* (London)

"Once again Father Martin gets to the heart of the matter, as evidenced in his book on building bridges between the Catholic Church and the LGBT community. Jesus prayed with deep passion that we might be one, and I believe that *Building a Bridge* goes a long way in helping to answer that prayer. Too often members of the LGBT community have been seen as 'other' when in fact together we are brothers and sisters, mothers and fathers, sons and daughters. As in any family, we are going to have our differences, but that does not make us any less family. This courageous work is necessary reading for all who wish to build up the Christian community and to give witness to the Gospel message of inclusion."

—John C. Wester, Archbishop of Santa Fe

"James Martin had to know, even before he typed a single word of *Building a Bridge* . . . that no matter what he wrote, he was walking into a minefield of criticism. Which makes his courage—and his compassion—even more powerful. . . . Martin counters [any] criticism with a simple, some might say unassailable, defense: 'Still, love is everyone's duty, because Jesus Christ calls for it.' He adds: 'For with Jesus, there is no us and them. There is only us.' The essential message here is long overdue: Martin urges the Catholic Church—and by extension, all believers in the gospel of love—to treat members of the LGBT community with 'respect, compassion, and sensitivity.' And in return, he asks the LGBT community to reciprocate, to treat the institutional church with those same core values. It's a proposition that shouldn't be radical."

—*Chicago Tribune*


"This is a bold book. It talks clearly and openly about an issue that daunts and taunts our church, and, in its well-reasoned way, it takes the hysterics out of the discussion. . . . We owe it to each other to build this bridge with the mutual 'respect, compassion, and sensitivity' that Martin describes."

—*America*


"I wanted to make sure that I affirmed what Father Martin was doing. . . . This is a priest who has given his life for the service of the church. He's been very dedicated; he's well-respected. The Holy Father appointed him to a commission in Rome. So, I would just say to people: Make up your own decision, your own mind about him, by reading exactly what he wrote. . . . He really is one of the foremost—if not the foremost—evangelizers in the church today, especially for young people."

—Cardinal Blase Cupich, Archbishop of Chicago

"Sexuality, gender, and religion—a volatile mix. With this book, Father Martin shows how the Rosary and the rainbow flag can peacefully meet each other. After this must-read you will understand why New Ways Ministry honored Father Martin with its Bridge Building Award."

—Sister Jeannine Gramick, SL, cofounder of New Ways Ministry and longtime LGBT advocate

"A recent book from Jesuit Father James Martin seems like an answer to a prayer. . . . Father Martin concludes his beautiful book with a selection of Scripture passages accompanied by questions for reflection both for gay readers and for their friends. It is well worth reading."

—Patrick Dunn, Bishop of Auckland, New Zealand

"The surprising places [in which] Martin finds insight highlight the subtlety of his thought and the time he has devoted to considering these questions. Although specifically Catholic, this approachable resource will resonate with many Christians looking for help with providing pastoral care to sexual minorities or living as an LGBTQ Christian."

—*Publishers Weekly*

"*Building a Bridge,* by Father James Martin, describes the 'culture of encounter' that Pope Francis frequently espouses. In order to construct this bridge, those on each side of the divide must presume the goodness and worth of the other and be motivated by the common desire to meet each other on the way. With a heart sympathetic to the suffering that LGBT people of faith have experienced and a love for the church, Father Martin describes how this encounter can be a fruitful and liberating journey for those on both sides."

—**John Stowe, Bishop of Lexington**

"It's still rare to find anyone in the church hierarchy today—especially a Catholic priest—who will speak frankly and favorably about the queer Catholic experience. Father James Martin is that rare exception, making it his mission to affirm their right to belong in the church."

—*Vice*

"A wonderful Jesuit, James Martin, has written a wonderful book in which he challenges the institutional church to be in dialogue with the

LGBT community. This has challenged a lot of people in the Catholic Church, because you don't want to build a bridge if you already think you're on the right side. But this is where we have to go next."

—Wilton D. Gregory, Archbishop of Atlanta

"If Martin's book, with its biblical reflections on God's loving creation of us and Jesus's unconditional welcome, can help LGBT people and our families experience and trust God's tenderness, he will have laid the foundation stone for social change and spiritual renewal."

—*The Washington Post*

"If you think a call to build bridges is a letdown because you wanted some more confrontational form of resistance, don't be fooled: being a peacemaker in this field is delicate and costly, and Father Martin, who has been building such bridges for many years, packs more of a punch than appears at first reading. He, like Pope Francis, knows that it is by drawing dangerously close and entering into relationships that we learn mercy, equality of heart, and love of enemies. If, and only if, we can be Christian in those things, then the scandal at the heart of the relationship between LGBT believers and our churches is well on the way to being undone."

—James Alison, author of *Faith Beyond Resentment: Fragments Catholic and Gay*

"Please read his book if you want to catch up on the constructions of this able bridge builder. Faithful Jesuit that he is, he frames these complex issues in larger contexts, and wants people on both sides to be connected by bridges and get to know each other as a first step."

—Reverend Martin E. Marty, professor emeritus of the history of modern Christianity at the University of Chicago

"The required two-way bridge must be built, Martin says, since 'respect, compassion, and sensitivity' that flows openly and intentionally in both directions. His book develops in more concrete ways what each of these terms might mean in such a dialogue. As it goes through specific tactics, approaches, and incidents, the book functions well as an extended examination of conscience for both sides in this often-bruising battle. . . . There is much to commend in the image of a two-way bridge in which such things are recognized, and the prerequisite for such recognition is the kind of reputation for respect, compassion, and sensitivity to all sides that Martin has justly earned."

—*Commonweal*

"In *Building a Bridge,* Father Martin urges a much-needed calm conversation among all Catholics and the LGBT community based on the full meaning of the Gospel teaching of love and respect for every human person. This book helps the whole church engage the mandate of Jesus to minister to all, not only without discrimination but with inclusive true love, which is due every child of God. I recommend it for parishes, schools, and family discussions."

—Joseph A. Fiorenza, Archbishop Emeritus of Galveston–Houston

"Martin's gentle, gracious, and attractive book...is not about sexual ethics but about ecclesiology and pastoral theology. The church is a pilgrim church, and its embrace should be inclusive."

—Lisa Sowle Cahill, *Theological Studies*

"It is recommended for prayer groups, Bible study groups, and book clubs, especially those at Catholic institutions ... as well as anyone who ministers to or teaches members of the LGBT community, their families and friends ... and members of the LGBT community, their families and friends."

—*Catholic Library World*

"In too many parts of our church LGBT people have been made to feel unwelcome, excluded, and even shamed. Father Martin's brave, prophetic, and inspiring book marks an essential step in inviting church leaders to minister with more compassion and in reminding LGBT Catholics that they are as much a part of our church as any other Catholic."

—Cardinal Joseph W. Tobin, Archbishop of Newark

# Building a Bridge

How the Catholic Church and the LGBT
Community Can Enter into a Relationship of
Respect, Compassion, and Sensitivity

Revised and Expanded Edition

JAMES MARTIN, SJ

HarperOne
*An Imprint of* HarperCollins*Publishers*

HarperOne

FIRST HARPERCOLLINS PAPERBACK EDITION PUBLISHED IN 2018

*Designed by SBI Book Arts, LLC*

Library of Congress Cataloging-in-Publication Data is available upon request.

ISBN 978-0-06-283753-0

20 21 22 LSC(H) 10 9 8 7

*Dedicated to all the LGBT people*
*and their families and friends*
*who have shared their joys and hopes*
*and their griefs and anxieties with me*

For it was you who formed
my inward parts;

you knit me together
in my mother's womb.

I praise you, for I am fearfully
and wonderfully made.

Wonderful are your works;
that I know very well.

(PSALM 139:13–14)

# Jesus of the Corners
## by Pádraig Ó Tuama

*Luke 7:44: "Then turning toward the
woman he said to Simon:
'Do you see this woman?' "*

*Jesus of the corners,*

*You saw all:
those at the centre
and those at the edge.*

*Guide us into all the corners
of our wide world,*

*Because when you went into rooms,
you found life and love
in the stories that others
ignored.*

*Amen.*

# CONTENTS

Introduction to the
Revised and Expanded Edition
1

Why I'm Writing
14

A Two-Way Bridge
27

Biblical Passages for Reflection
and Meditation
109

A Prayer for When I Feel Rejected
167

Questions for Book Groups
and Personal Reflection
173

Acknowledgments
189

# Introduction to
# the Revised and
# Expanded Edition

Since the first edition of *Building a Bridge* was published, I've been happy to have the opportunity to speak at many parishes, colleges, retreat houses, and conventions, as well as one-on-one with many LGBT people, their parents and grandparents, brothers and sisters, and friends and neighbors. Many of these encounters have been deeply moving, since so many people have shared their personal stories with me—stories about suffering and struggle, about perseverance and hope, and about doubt and faith.

With every encounter, I have learned something new. At the same time, I've also spoken with cardinals, bishops, priests, and other church officials, including lay pastoral associates and parish workers, about their reactions to the book.

All these conversations, as well as reviews of the book, letters from readers, and messages received through social media, encouraged me to expand this book and incorporate the insights I've learned along the way.

Let me mention five specific insights that have proven helpful.

*First,* shortly after the book's publication, I realized something that may not be surprising for some readers: ministry to LGBT people is a ministry not simply to the relatively small percentage of Catholics who are LGBT but to a much larger group.

Initially, the book was intended for two distinct audiences: LGBT Catholics and church officials. But after almost every talk, lecture, or retreat, people would say something like "My daughter is lesbian and hasn't gone to church in years, and I'm looking forward to giving her your book." Parents, in particular, sought me out to tell me their stories, which were always edifying and educational. Beyond that, I've heard from grandparents, aunts and uncles, brothers and sisters, nieces and nephews, as well as neighbors, friends, roommates, coworkers, and on and on.

Thus, far more people than I had anticipated are touched by this topic. And the number is only growing. As more Catholics feel comfortable sharing their sexuality and identity, more Catholic families are affected by LGBT issues. And as more families carry their hopes and desires into their parishes, more priests and pastoral workers are affected. In turn, more bishops and diocesan officials are affected. In such gradual ways, the entire church is affected.

The first realization, then, was that ministry to LGBT Catholics is ministry not just to LGBT people but, increasingly, to the entire church. Likewise, while this book is written primarily for Catholics, I hope it will prove helpful to all Christians who seek to welcome LGBT people in their churches.

*Second,* I realized that I needed to be clearer about one specific topic: where the onus for the bridge building lies. The first edition of this book expressed that obliquely but not directly, because I thought it was obvious.

So let me say it more clearly: the institutional church bears the main responsibility for the ministry of dialogue and reconciliation, because it is the institutional church that has made LGBT Catholics feel marginalized, not the other way around. It is true that the public actions of a few LGBT groups have targeted the institutional church, and provoked strong reactions, but in terms of making people feel marginalized, it is the clergy and other church officials who bear responsibility.

*Third,* a few readers wondered why I seemed to have left out two things from the book: a discussion about the church's teachings on same-sex relations and same-sex marriage, and a discussion about the sexual abuse crisis in the church.

That last topic—sexual abuse—was covered only glancingly in the first edition. Some asked why I didn't discuss the topic in depth, since it was an important reason why many LGBT people have left the church, mainly because they felt some church leaders were hypocritical in criticizing their sexual activity while countenancing sexual abuse by the clergy. (In the first edition, as here, I quote a gay man who expresses that feeling.) That sentiment, of course, is shared by many straight people as well.

But I intentionally did not include a discussion of the

clergy abuse crisis and the crimes of sexual abuse not because I am afraid to tackle that topic (I've written about it elsewhere) but for another reason: that critical topic deserved a far more comprehensive treatment than was possible in a short book. I didn't want to address it because it warrants an exhaustive treatment beyond the scope of this book.

The omission of a long discussion on same-sex relations was also intentional, because the Catholic Church's stance on the matter is clear: sexual relations between people of the same sex are impermissible. At the same time, the LGBT Catholic community's stance on the matter is also clear: same-sex relations are part and parcel of their lives. (Here I am speaking about the majority of LGBT Catholics, not the relatively small portion of the group who think otherwise.) Theologically speaking, you could argue that this teaching has not been "received" by the LGBT Catholic community, to whom it was primarily directed.

So I intentionally decided not to discuss that question at any length, since it is an area on which the two sides are simply too far apart. The same holds true for same-sex marriage: it is an issue on which the institutional church and most of the LGBT community are too far apart. In this edition, I quote the *Catechism*'s entire teaching on LGBT sexuality (more specifically, on homosexuality), but again I don't enter into a lengthy discussion because I prefer to focus on areas of possible commonality.

Likewise, this book is not a treatise on moral theology, nor is it a reflection on the sexual morality of LGBT people. I am not a moral theologian. Moreover, not everything has to be about sex. This is a book primarily about dialogue and prayer.

*Fourth,* I would like to address the question of hate. While the vast majority of readers—particularly LGBT people and their families—expressed gratitude for the book, often with great emotion, the book unleashed in a few quarters of the church a virtual torrent of hate. Most of these expressions of intolerance appeared on social media, but in other venues as well I saw how the mere idea of welcoming LGBT people gave rise to the most homophobic and hateful comments you can imagine. Of course I expected some criticism of the book, and I invited discussion in the first edition, but the intensity of the hate took me by surprise.

For the most part, I could anticipate the more thoughtful critical reactions: some LGBT Catholics would say that I had not gone far enough; some bishops and church officials would say that I had gone too far. But critical reactions are to be expected. This is the nature of dialogue and the nature of inviting people into a conversation—onto the bridge, if you will.

Much of the criticism and discussion has been helpful, constructive, and challenging in the best way. And I've learned a great deal from my critics. Many of their questions guided me in writing this new edition.

Some of the criticism, however, has been neither helpful nor constructive: some of it has been, as I said, hateful. It serves as a vivid reminder of how much homophobia still exists in society and in the church. And a reminder of how treacherous the waters are underneath the bridge. Sometimes it was hard to keep up with the attacks online, but the hateful comments and personal attacks were always put in perspective after just a few minutes with LGBT Catholics and their family members. Just a few tears from an LGBT Catholic more than made up for an ocean of hateful attacks.

Where does this anger come from? From several places, I would suggest:

a) A fear of the LGBT person as the "other," the person who is seen as different and whose differences are seen as a threat. This is true "homophobia," that is, actual fear of the LGBT person.

b) A hatred of the LGBT person as the "other." This illustrates the more colloquial way of using the term "homophobia," meaning not fear but hatred. This hatred is sometimes transformed into scape-goating, where the LGBT person is viewed primarily, or only, through the lens of sin, when, in fact, we are all sinners.

c) A disgust or revulsion over the idea of same-sex relations or of same-sex attraction. This sometimes leads to a hatred of the LGBT person.

These three preceding reasons (fear, hatred, and revulsion) often lead to not only anger, but a kind of schoolyard bullying—name-calling, personal vilification, and even threats of violence.

d) A fear that any attempt to "build a bridge," to listen to the experiences of people previously seen as "other," or to encourage people to reflect on church practices in a new way is tantamount to advocating a complete change in church teaching. It is not, of course, but opposition to building bridges for that reason sometimes solidifies into general opposition and transforms into anger.

To that end, it's important for Catholic readers to know that this book has the formal ecclesiastical approval of my Jesuit superior. That is, as required of all books published by Jesuits, the manuscript was vetted by my Jesuit province's *Censor Librorum* (the censor of books) and then received official approval for publication (the *Imprimi Potest* in the front of the book) from my Jesuit Provincial Superior. It has also been endorsed by several cardinals, archbishops, and bishops. So everything in this book begins with the Gospels, builds on the *Catechism of the Catholic Church*, and is well within church teaching.

e) A fear that welcoming those people on the margins is what Jesus would want. Here the fear—usually from those who know the Gospels well—is not that offering welcome to those people seen as "other" is wrong but, rather, that it is precisely what Jesus did. While it is easy to oppose, say, same-sex marriage because it's against a traditional view of marriage, it's harder to argue that Jesus did not offer welcome to people on the margins. Frustration flows from the recognition that the inclusion of LGBT people is entirely consistent with Jesus's practice of including the marginalized. This cognitive dissonance between opposing marginalized people and knowing that Jesus welcomed them can produce anger in some people, as they struggle with that fierce internal tension.

f) A discomfort with one's own sexuality. Since the book was first published, I have spoken to many friends who are practicing psychologists and psychiatrists, and they all point to this as one of the most important factors in explaining the intense anger. Human sexuality is complex, and all of us, say psychiatrists and psychologists, are on a kind of spectrum in terms of which gender we are attracted to. Some of us are uncomfortable with that, and so raising topics like homosexuality terrifies us because it forces us to confront those complicated feelings. This terror is more easily directed outward, and can take the form of anger.

For the most part, however, I've not been overly bothered by the anger, the invectives, or even the personal attacks, since the book was meant to start a conversation, not to serve as the final word on the topic. The attacks also served an important purpose: to remind me why this was an important topic to discuss and why it was important to advocate for LGBT Catholics who long to find a place in their church.

*Fifth,* and on a far more positive note, I underestimated the desire for conversation around LGBT Catholics within the church itself. One of the first talks I gave after the book's publication was at Saint Cecilia Church in Boston—a parish well known for its welcome of LGBT people—drawing over seven hundred people, who packed the church on a weekday night.

The size of the crowd shocked me. At the time, coming off a few months of writing the book, I was, unsurprisingly, so immersed in it that I considered the book rather mild. But seeing a packed church made me realize that for many people this was something new. For many Catholics, seeing and hearing a priest speak on these issues prompted deep emotional reactions. Young LGBT people hugged me, parents and grandparents of LGBT children wept, and people told me, in stronger terms than I could ever have anticipated, how grateful they were.

A gay friend echoed this, in an email sent to me after one of these events: "I suspect one of the reasons this is so powerful for many Catholics is because a priest is saying it. Most people aren't around priests that often, usually for just an hour or on Sundays. So when it comes to LGBT issues and the clergy, most Catholics only hear the negative voices that are loudest or highlighted by the media. Seeing a priest say the things you say is a powerful counter-narrative. Having a member of the clergy say something positive about LGBT people is both novel and powerful."

That's likely true. But also likely is that these reactions were not simply about hearing a priest say these things, or about this book (for many of them had not yet read it), but about something even deeper: the simple desire for an open discussion of this topic, which had for so long only been whispered about. I was often reminded of Jesus's words in the Gospel of Matthew: "What I say to you in the dark, tell in the light; and what you hear whispered, proclaim from the housetops" (10:27).

This was confirmed time and again. A few weeks later, at the Church of Saint Paul the Apostle in New York City, I gave an evening talk. Not only had I spoken on the topic a few weeks prior at the church, but also the parish is well known for its vibrant LGBT outreach program. Consequently, I thought few would attend the talk. But again, it attracted a standing-room-only crowd, and the event went over the allotted time since there were so many questions to be fielded. Not long afterwards, I spoke at Villanova University in suburban Philadelphia. Again, I assumed that at a Catholic university in a well-heeled part of the country, the discussion would be superfluous. But again, we had over seven hundred people—students, parents, people from around the area—in a packed church. After both events, attendees waited for up to two hours to share their stories with me, often with great emotion.

These were all reminders of the need for discussion—even in places where the topic seems "known." One of the final questions at Saint Paul's was "What can we do next?"

There is a deep and evident desire for bridges to be built in our church.

*Finally,* this book is not an argument, not a polemic, not a debate, but an invitation to conversation and prayer, and then to a ministry rooted in Jesus Christ. Every Christian ministry is rooted in Jesus, but to reach out to those who feel on the margins is to follow Jesus most closely. For this was one of his primary tasks, and so it should be for the church.

So I'm happy to continue this ministry with this revised and expanded edition. May it lead to a continuing of the conversation, a building of bridges, and a growing spirit of respect, compassion, and sensitivity.

# Why I'm Writing

In the summer of 2016, a gunman stormed into a nightclub popular among the gay community in Orlando, Florida, and killed forty-nine people. It was, at that time, the largest mass shooting in U.S. history.

In response, millions in this country, myself included, grieved and voiced their support for the LGBT (lesbian, gay, bisexual, and transgender) community. But I was also concerned by what I did not hear. Although some church leaders expressed both sorrow and horror, only a handful of the more than two hundred fifty Catholic bishops used the terms *gay* or *LGBT*. Cardinal Blase Cupich of Chicago; Bishop Robert Lynch of Saint Petersburg, Florida; Bishop David Zubik of Pittsburgh; Bishop Robert McElroy of San Diego; and Bishop John Stowe of Lexington, Kentucky, all spoke out strongly in support of the LGBT community or against homophobia within days of the shooting. Many more, however, remained silent.

I found this revelatory. The fact that only a few Catholic bishops acknowledged the LGBT community or even used the word *gay* during such a critical time showed that the LGBT community is still invisible in many quarters of the church. Even in tragedy, its members are invisible.

This event helped me to recognize something in a new way: the work of the Gospel cannot be accomplished if one part of the church is essentially separated from any other part. Between the two groups—the LGBT community and the institutional church—a great chasm has formed, a separation for which a bridge needs to be built.

For many years, I've ministered to and worked with LGBT people, most of them Catholics. My ministry has not been primarily through classes or seminars but rather through more informal channels. Gay, lesbian, bisexual, and transgender people as well as their parents and friends have come to me for advice, counsel, confession, and spiritual direction. After Masses, lectures, or retreats, they will ask advice on spiritual and religious matters, pose questions on church-related issues, or simply share their experiences.

During these times, I've listened to their joys and hopes, their griefs and anxieties, sometimes accompanied by tears, sometimes by laughter. In the process, I've become friends with many of them. A great many bishops, priests, deacons, sisters, brothers, and lay pastoral workers in the church could say the same thing.

I've also worked with and come to know many cardinals, archbishops, bishops, and other church officials and leaders. After thirty years as a Jesuit and twenty years working for a Catholic media ministry, I've become friendly with members of the hierarchy through a variety of ways, from Masses to pilgrimages to speaking events to retreats to dinner-table conversations. These church leaders are my friends and I rely on their wise counsel and pastoral support.

Over the years, I've discovered a great divide. I lament that there isn't greater understanding and more conversation between LGBT Catholics and the institutional church. I would rather not refer to two "sides," since everyone is part of the church. But many LGBT Catholics have told me that they have felt hurt by the institutional church—unwelcomed, excluded, and insulted.

At the same time, many in the institutional church want to reach out to this community but often seem confused about how to do so. Yes, it seems that there are some who don't seem to want to reach out and some who even seem hostile to LGBT people, but the bishops I know are sincere in their desire for pastoral outreach.

For the past three decades as a Jesuit, part of my ministry has been, informally, trying to build bridges between these groups. But after the shooting in Orlando, my desire to do so in a more formal way intensified.

So when New Ways Ministry, a group that ministers to and advocates for LGBT Catholics, asked a few weeks after the Orlando tragedy if I would accept their Bridge Building Award and give a talk at the award ceremony, I agreed. The name of the award inspired me to sketch out an idea for a "two-way bridge" that might help bring together the institutional church and the LGBT community.

The first half of this book is that talk, which has been expanded into a longer essay. The essay urges the church to treat the LGBT community with "respect, compassion, and sensitivity" (a phrase from the *Catechism of the Catholic Church*) and the LGBT community to reciprocate, reflecting those virtues in its own relationship with the institutional church.

Let me say something important at the outset. I understand the difficulties that LGBT people have faced in the church. They have shared stories with me about being insulted, slandered, excluded, rejected, and even fired. I don't want to minimize that pain.

Recently, for example, I received a message from a woman in the United States, asking me if I knew a "compassionate priest" living anywhere near her. She was working in a hospice, and the local priest assigned to care for patients was refusing to anoint a man who was on the verge of death—because he was gay. So I hope I can begin to appreciate the tremendous pain LGBT people have felt at the hands of some of the church's ministers.

Still, I believe it's important for the LGBT community—for everyone, in fact—to treat others with respect, even when their own church at times feels like an enemy. That is part of being a Christian, hard as it is.

This does not mean that one cannot critique and challenge the church when it needs to be critiqued and challenged. But all of that can be done with respect, compassion, and sensitivity. In fact, respect, compassion, and sensitivity are undervalued gifts for dealing with conflict and disagreement in general, gifts that can be shared with the wider culture. These virtues can help not only Catholics and Christians but all people of good-will who seek unity.

In recent years, the overall social and political climate in the United States has become more divisive and social discourse more contentious. Even abroad, various social, political, and ethnic groups find themselves pitted against one another with an intensity that seems not only new but frightening. Not too long ago, opposing factions would often interact with one another politely and work together for the common good. Certainly there were tensions, but a quiet courtesy and tacit respect prevailed. Now all one seems to find is contempt. As a result, many people feel powerless to prevent the continued fraying of the social fabric as well as the name-calling, personal attacks, and violence that such division gives rise to.

For me, the echo chambers created by social media in which one's worldview is barely challenged, the news channels specializing in simplistic and sometimes false analyses of complicated political situations, and the civic leaders seemingly unconcerned about the division their words and actions might cause are all developments that contribute to this disunity, as well as to the feelings of hopelessness that arise in the face of this disunity.

In these times, the church should be a sign of unity. Frankly, in all times. Yet many people see the church as contributing to division, as some Christian leaders and their congregations mark off boundaries of "us" and "them." But the church works best when it embodies the virtues of respect, compassion, and sensitivity.

So I hope this brief book might be a meditation for

the church at large, not simply for those people inter-ested in LGBT issues.

⟨❦ ❦⟩

A few notes.

First of all, not every church leader needs to be up-braided for not treating LGBT Catholics with care. Far from it. Besides the bishops I've already mentioned, there are dozens more who are warm and welcoming to the LGBT community, and there are plenty of parishes with vibrant outreach programs to this community. Many bishops and priests—to say nothing of deacons, sisters and brothers, and Catholic lay leaders—should be praised for their compassionate ministry to LGBT Catholics.

In fact, one of the most surprising aspects of the church for non-Catholics is how much ministry to the LGBT community goes on, in quiet and unheralded ways, in so many dioceses and parishes. Many LGBT Catholics love their parishes and feel very much at home there.

Second, not every LGBT person struggles with self-acceptance; these days the process of coming to under-stand one's identity as an LGBT person is easier than it was just a few decades ago.

For example, one of the most moving parts of the

gathering at New Ways Ministry in Baltimore was being accompanied by two friends: one, a young man, age sixteen, who had just revealed to classmates at his Catholic high school that he was gay; and the other, his father, in his late forties, who had, along with the rest of his family, accepted his son with open arms and an open heart. And the very next weekend, on a trip to Philadelphia for a parish talk, I was given a ride from the train station by two brothers, both in their twenties. One of them, a college student, spontaneously told me that he was gay, and his relaxed manner quickly telegraphed his complete comfort with his sexuality.

So I don't wish to imply by my comments, or by the biblical passages appearing in this book, that an LGBT person *should* feel excluded. Some LGBT people simply presume, as they should, their place in the church and aren't bothered by the stray negative comments they hear. For most LGBT people, however, the process of understanding that they are loved by God as they are, and the process of finding their place in the church, remain difficult.

Third, though the book invites both groups—the institutional church and LGBT Catholics—to approach each other with respect, compassion, and sensitivity, the onus for this process lies on the institutional church. The main burden for this bridge building falls on bishops, priests, and other church officials, who are invited to take the first steps and work harder at reconciliation. Why? Because, as I've mentioned, even though a few LGBT groups have publicly targeted the church, it is the institutional church that has made LGBT Catholics feel marginalized, not the other way around.

By the way, my use of *LGBT* as an adjective is not meant to exclude anyone; this is the most common nomenclature at the time that I'm writing. One could also use LGBTQ (lesbian, gay, bisexual, transgender, and questioning or queer) or LGBTQA (lesbian, gay, bisexual, transgender, questioning or queer, and asexual) or LGBT+. Perhaps someday we will settle on a shorter acronym or an all-inclusive name, but my goal is to include all people who feel that their spiritual journey and their welcome in the church have been made more difficult by their sexual orientation or gender identity.

Overall, I'd like to offer a bridge for all of us, and then offer further support for that bridge with the second half of the book: a series of biblical passages that have proven helpful for LGBT Catholics, as well as brief reflections on those passages. Some of these are mentioned in the first half of the book—like the stories of Jesus's healing

of the Roman centurion's servant and Jesus's encounter
with Zacchaeus, the chief tax collector in Jericho. At
first blush, you might wonder what these familiar passages could possibly say to LGBT people, but when you
see the story through new eyes, I hope it will become
clearer.

I have also included other biblical passages that, based
on my experience, have proven the most helpful in the
spiritual journeys of LGBT Catholics. These too will be
accompanied by brief reflections and questions as an aid
to praying with those passages.

These select biblical passages and my own reflections
are also meant for LGBT parents, friends, allies, and the
entire church—including parishes and dioceses, priests
and bishops. The Bible, after all, is for everyone. I hope
these reflections might be of help on both the personal
level and the communal level, to invite parishes and dioceses into communal prayer, conversation, discernment,
and action. And conversion.

The term *conversion* in this context deserves some attention. In fact, I use the term so often in my Jesuit life
that I sometimes forget the word may carry a different
meaning for LGBT people and their friends and families.
What I mean by *conversion* is the conversion that *all of us*
are called to by God and the conversion of minds and
hearts that Jesus called for.

In the Gospel of Mark, one of the first things Jesus does is call for *metanoia*, which is often translated as "repentance" but is probably more accurately translated as "conversion" (Mk. 1:15). Remember that while Jesus would have preached mostly in Aramaic, his native tongue, the Gospels were written in Greek. *Meta* is the Greek for "after" or "beyond" and *nous* is "mind." In Jesus's time, a *metanoia* meant a transformative change in one's mind and heart.

Thus, I do not mean that the only people called to conversion are LGBT people, or that they are called to "conversion therapy," a debunked set of methodologies that tries to "change" LGBT people into straight people. Conversion—*metanoia*—is for everyone.

Finally, I know this subject—the treatment of LGBT people in the church and the church's outreach to them—is a highly sensitive one for many people. Because I have met and ministered to LGBT people, I know each situation is unique and these situations can be imbued with great anguish.

So I apologize if anyone feels I am minimizing their pain, misunderstanding their situation, needlessly scolding them, or leaving out something important. My experience with LGBT people is lengthy, but it is certainly not as extensive as that of others who work in this ministry directly.

This essay, then, is not a complete blueprint for the bridge, with detailed instructions for its building, or a bolt-by-bolt survey of the final construction. Rather, it is a preliminary sketch, a starting point, an occasion for conversation and reflection. Feel free to disagree—as people have already. And please reflect on what you find helpful in this book and leave the rest behind.

So, my friends, I invite you to join me on a bridge.

# A Two-Way Bridge

The relationship between LGBT Catholics and the Catholic Church has been at times contentious and combative and at times warm and welcoming. Much of the tension characterizing this complicated relationship results from a lack of communication and a good deal of mistrust between LGBT Catholics and the hierarchy. What is needed is a bridge between that community and the church.

So I would like to invite you to walk with me as I describe how we might build that bridge. To that end, I would like to reflect on both the church's outreach to the LGBT community and the LGBT community's outreach to the church, because good bridges take people in both directions.

As you probably know, the *Catechism of the Catholic Church* says that Catholics are called to treat homosexuals with "respect, compassion, and sensitivity" (No. 2358). What might that mean? Let's meditate on that question, and on a second question as well: What might it mean for the LGBT community to treat the church with respect, compassion, and sensitivity?

To answer this, it may be helpful to define these two groups. Of course, LGBT people are part of the church, so in a sense those questions imply a false dichotomy. The church is the entire "People of God," to use the language of the Second Vatican Council. So it may seem strange to discuss how the People of God can relate to a part of the People of God. In good Jesuit fashion, then, let me refine our terms.

When I refer to the church in this discussion, I mean the "institutional church"—that is, the Vatican and the church hierarchy (popes and cardinals, archbishops and bishops, priests and deacons) as well as anyone, including laymen and laywomen, who works in any sort of official capacity in the church. In essence, these are the decision-makers in our church. So for purposes of this discussion the "institutional church" includes not only the pope but also the laywoman who is the principal of a Catholic high school. Also, I will at times refer to both LGBT Catholics and the LGBT community. In fact, the church has relationships with both groups, because what it says about LGBT Catholics often reaches the ears of LGBT people who are not Catholic.

Let's begin by taking a walk on the first lane of the bridge, the one leading from the institutional church to the LGBT community, and reflect on what it might mean for the church to treat LGBT people with respect, compassion, and sensitivity.

# Respect

First of all, *respect* means, at the very least, recognizing that the LGBT community *exists,* and extending to it the same recognition that any community desires and deserves because of its presence among us.

In the wake of the Orlando tragedy in 2016, some church leaders spoke of the event without ever mentioning the terms *LGBT* or *gay.* This revealed a certain failure to acknowledge the existence of this community. But this is not a Christian model, for Jesus recognizes all people, even those who seem invisible in the greater community. In fact, he reaches out specifically to people on the margins. Catholics, therefore, have a responsibility to make everyone feel visible and valuable.

Recognizing that LGBT Catholics exist has important pastoral implications. It means carrying out ministries to this community, which some dioceses, parishes, and schools already do well. Examples include celebrating Masses with LGBT groups, sponsoring diocesan and parish outreach programs, and in general helping LGBT Catholics feel that they are part of the church, that they are welcomed and loved.

Some Catholics have objected to this approach, saying that any outreach implies a tacit agreement with everything anyone in the LGBT community says or does. But this is an unfair objection because it is raised with virtually no other group. If a diocese sponsors, for example, an outreach group for Catholic business leaders, it does not mean that the diocese agrees with every value of corporate America. Nor does it mean that the church has sanctified everything every businessman or businesswoman says or does. No one suggests that. Why not? Because people understand that the diocese is trying to help the members of that group feel more connected to their church, the church they belong to, by virtue of their baptism.

Let me pause here to underline the importance of baptism in light of this discussion. "Holy Baptism is the basis of the whole Christian life," says the *Catechism* in a marvelous phrase, "the gateway to life in the Spirit"

(No. 1213). Its importance cannot be overestimated. Baptism incorporates us into the church.

It is essential for all Christians, including LGBT Catholics, to grasp the significance of this sacrament in their lives and how it seals their place in the church.

Not long ago, at the start of a Sunday Mass at my local parish in New York City, the presider announced that there would be a baptism. The priest did a fine job of weaving the baptismal rite into the larger context of the Mass, and at the appointed moment, he pronounced the ancient formula, "I baptize you, Ellie, in the name of the Father and of the Son and of the Holy Spirit," as he poured water over the child's head. Then he held the child aloft and said, "Welcome to the Christian community!"

At that moment, the church organ boomed out the first few notes of the Easter hymn "The Strife is O'er," which begins with a loud "Alleluia! Alleluia! Alleluia!"

And I thought, *Yes! This is a life-changing moment, for the child, for the family, for the church, and for the entire universe. A new person has been welcomed into the church. The heavens are indeed shouting "Alleluia!"*

Immediately I thought of LGBT people and how often people tell them that they don't belong in the church. But Christ himself called them into the church—forever. So when LGBT people report that someone has told them they are not part of the church, I often say, "You were baptized. You have as much of a place in your church as the pope, your local bishop, or me."

Part of respect is treating LGBT Catholics as full members of the church, by virtue of their baptism.

Second, *respect* means calling a group what it asks to be called. On a personal level, if someone says, "I prefer to be called Jim instead of James," you would naturally listen and call him by the name he prefers. It's common courtesy.

It's the same on a group level. We don't use the antiquated and even offensive term "Negroes" any longer. Why? Because that group feels more comfortable with other names, like "African Americans" or "blacks." Recently, I was told that "disabled persons" is not as acceptable as "people with disabilities." So now I use the latter term. Why? Because it is respectful to call people by the name they choose. Everyone has a right to the name they wish to be called by.

This is not a minor concern. In the Jewish and Christian traditions, names are important. In the Old Testament, God gives Adam and Eve the authority to name the creatures (Gen. 2:18–23). God also renames Abram as

Abraham (Gen. 17:4–6). A name in the Hebrew Scriptures stands for a person's identity; knowing a person's name meant, in a sense, that you knew the person, that you had a certain intimacy with the person, even that you possessed a kind of power over the person. That is one reason why, when Moses asks to know God's name, God says, "I am who I am" (Exod. 3:14–15)—in other words, as my Old Testament professor explained to our class, "None of your business."

Later, in the New Testament, Jesus renames Simon as Peter (Matt. 16:18; Jn. 1:42). The persecutor Saul renames himself as Paul (Acts 13:9). Names are important in our church today as well. The first question a priest or deacon asks the parents at an infant's baptism in the Catholic Church is "What name do you give this child?"

Because names are important, church leaders are invited to be attentive to how they name the LGBT community. So let us lay to rest antiquated phrases like "afflicted with same-sex attraction," which no LGBT person I know uses, and even "homosexual person," which seems overly clinical to many. Besides, how will the LGBT community be able to listen if the church persists in using language offensive to their ears?

On this topic, as on all topics, we can look to Jesus for guidance.

Think about the ways in which Jesus spoke to the

people of his time. Especially as recorded in the Synoptic Gospels (Matthew, Mark, and Luke), Jesus used language his followers could understand, words and phrases tailored to their own situations.

When he first meets the disciples who are fishing by the Sea of Galilee, for example, he doesn't speak to them as a carpenter would—by saying, "Let us construct the house of God" or "Let us lay the foundations of the reign of God."

Instead, Jesus the carpenter speaks to them in *their* language, the language of fishermen: "Follow me," he says, "and I will make you fish for people" (Mk. 1:16–20; Matt. 4:18–22).

Dialogue begins by recognizing how to speak with another person. We need to be especially attentive to this with the LGBT community. As the U.S. Conference of Catholic Bishops says in their pastoral letter *Always Our Children,* written in 1997 and addressed to the parents of LGBT Catholics, "Language should not be a barrier to building trust and honest communication."

There is also an overlooked irony here: the term "same-sex attraction" is the one currently favored by some traditionalist Catholics, who object to using "gay" or "LGBT" because those terms supposedly identify a person only by their sexual urges. But this is precisely what the term "same-sex attraction" does. And, for good measure, "same-sex attraction" includes the word "sex." By that yardstick, it is hardly an improvement. I have always wondered if the resistance to "gay" and "LGBT" stems from the fact that these terms are the ones preferred by LGBT people, and so using them is considered a form of "caving."

I'm not the only one who supports calling people by the names they choose. In 2017, Cardinal Blase Cupich, the archbishop of Chicago, said, in response to a question at a public lecture:

> We have always wanted to make sure that we start the conversation by saying that all people are of value and their lives should be respected and that we should respect them. That is why I think that the terms "gay" and "lesbian" and "LGBT," all of those names that people appropriate to themselves, should be respected. People should be called the way that they want to be called rather than us coming up with terms that maybe we're more comfortable with. So it begins with that.

Let us, then, lay to rest phrases that no one in the LGBT community uses. Instead let's listen to what our gay brothers and lesbian sisters and transgender siblings prefer to name themselves. Instead of prescribing what names to use, though "gay," "lesbian," "LGBT," and "LGBTQ" are among the most common, I invite church leaders to recognize that people have a right to name themselves. Using those names is part of respect.

And if Pope Francis, and several of his cardinals and bishops, can use the word *gay*, as they have done several times during his papacy, so can the rest of the church.

*Respect* also means acknowledging that LGBT Catholics bring unique gifts to the church—both as individuals and as a community. These gifts build up the church in special ways, as Saint Paul wrote when he compared the People of God to a human body (1 Cor. 12:12–27). Each body part is important: the hand, the eye, the foot. In fact, as Paul said, it is the parts of the body that "we think less honorable" that deserve even greater respect.

Many LGBT people have indeed felt "less honorable" in the church. At a recent parish talk the moderator asked all the LGBT Catholics in the room to raise their hands. A forest of hands went up. Then he said, "How many of you have ever felt excluded in the church?" Not one hand was lowered.

Following Saint Paul, it is to these beloved members and to their great gifts that we should pay even *greater* respect. "Those members of the body that we think less honorable we clothe with greater honor," he wrote.

Consider the many gifts brought by LGBT Catholics who work in parishes, schools, chanceries, retreat centers, hospitals, and social service agencies. Let us "honor" them, as Saint Paul says. To take several examples, some of the most gifted music ministers I have known in my almost thirty years as a Jesuit have been gay men who have brought tremendous joy to their parishes, week in and week out, during every liturgical season. For several years, I worked with a lesbian woman in a Jesuit ministry who brought immense reserves of smarts, talent, and good humor to the job. One of my favorite spiritual directors—that is, people who help you notice the presence of God in your prayer and your daily life—was a gay man. Another was a lesbian. Their wise counsel and patient listening helped me more than I can express. Faithful, thoughtful, intelligent, committed, and loving LGBT people have enriched my spiritual life in countless ways.

The whole church is invited to meditate on how LGBT Catholics build up the church with their presence, in the same way that elderly people, teenagers, women, people with disabilities, various ethnic groups, or any other groups build up a parish or a diocese. And although it is usually wrong to generalize, we can still pose the question: What might those gifts be?

Many, if not most, LGBT people have endured, from an early age, misunderstanding, prejudice, hatred, persecution, and even violence, and therefore often feel a natural compassion toward the marginalized. *Their compassion* is a gift. They have often been made to feel unwelcome in their parishes and in their church, but they persevere because of their vigorous faith. *Their perseverance* is a gift. They are often forgiving of clergy and other church employees who have treated them like damaged goods. Their *forgiveness* is a gift. Compassion, perseverance, and forgiveness are all gifts.

One could add gifts that are applicable to more specific ministries. Recently, a woman who works with people with physical disabilities told me that she believed LGBT people make some of the best outreach workers with that population. Why? As a social worker, she surmised this: "LGBT people have been judged for so long that they approach people in ministry free of any judgment." In her experience, many people tend to judge those with physical disabilities. LGBT people, in her experience, seemed freer of a reflexive need to judge.

LGBT Catholics are also some of the most effective evangelists for Catholicism in their communities. At a parish talk, a lesbian woman who was asked to respond to my lecture drew appreciative laughs from the crowd when she said that the most difficult challenge was not coming out as a lesbian to her Catholic friends but "coming out as a Catholic to her lesbian friends." She serves as a kind of ambassador for Catholicism to her LGBT friends, some of whom harbor suspicions about the church. For her, however, it is a home. At the same time, she helps the church reflect on the place of LGBT people in its midst. Another lesbian friend of mine called this process "double evangelization."

Let me add another gift: that of celibate priests and brothers who are gay, as well as chaste members of men's and women's religious orders who are gay or lesbian.

Now, there are many reasons why almost no gay clergy, and almost no gay and lesbian members of religious orders, are public about their sexuality. Among these reasons are the following: they are private people; their bishops or religious superiors ask them not to speak about it publicly; they themselves are uncomfortable with their sexuality; or they fear reprisals from parishioners or those with whom they minister.

But there are hundreds, perhaps thousands, of holy and hardworking gay clergy, and gay and lesbian members of religious orders, who live out their promises of celibacy and vows of chastity and help to build up the church.

Sometimes my mentioning this surprises people. Or angers them. But I am not saying anything polemical; I am merely stating a fact: I know many celibate gay priests, chaste gay brothers, and chaste lesbian sisters. At times, they have been my spiritual directors, my confessors, even my religious superiors. Some of them are the holiest people I have ever met. Saying that I know them is like saying that I see the sun in the sky. It's a simple fact.

These men and women freely give their whole selves to the church. They themselves are the gift.

Seeing, naming, and honoring all these gifts are components of respecting our LGBT brothers and sisters. So too is accepting them as beloved children of God and *letting them know* that they are beloved children of God. The church has a special call to proclaim God's love for a people who are often made to feel—whether by their families, neighbors, or religious leaders—as though they were damaged goods, unworthy of ministry, and even subhuman. The church is invited to both proclaim and demonstrate that LGBT people are beloved children of God.

꧁ ꧂

It is also important to remember that LGBT people are, like all of us, called to holiness. "Holiness" is a word that is not used enough about LGBT people, but the Second Vatican Council spoke about the "universal call to holiness," everyone's call to sanctity (*Lumen Gentium*, 5). As Saint Teresa of Calcutta liked to say, holiness is everyone's duty. And everyone's joy, I would add.

LGBT people are called to be holy, as all of us are.

We need, therefore, also to consider the fact that some of the saints were probably gay, lesbian, or bisexual. Yes, I know those terms weren't used until recently, and the modern concept of homosexuality is a relatively late cultural construct, but if a certain small percentage of human beings are gay, lesbian, or bisexual, then it stands to reason that a certain small percentage of the thousands of saints were as well—because they are, of course, human beings. And holiness makes it home in humanity.

In other words, among the saints were some men and women who were attracted to people of the same sex. That's not to say that they acted on their sexual desires, but if you consider—to take just one example among the thousands of saints—the many priests, brothers, and sisters who have been canonized, it's likely that some of them, even as they faithfully lived out their promises of celibacy and vows of chastity, experienced attractions to people of the same sex.

Which ones? It's hard to say. Perhaps impossible to

say, given how little homosexuality would have been understood, admitted to, and discussed in the past. To my mind, though, there are some saints who, at least based on their writings and what we know about their lives, seem to have been what we would today call gay or lesbian. But again, it's difficult to know for sure.

In our own time, we can look to several well-known holy persons who were also LGBT. As should be obvious by now, I've known many holy LGBT people in my life. In a more public vein, think of someone like Mychal Judge, OFM, the Franciscan fire chaplain and hero of the 9/11 attacks. Father Judge was the first official victim of the attacks in New York City, after he selflessly rushed into one of the Twin Towers at the World Trade Center to minister to the rescue workers, and was killed. He was also a celibate gay priest. How do I know he was gay? Not only based on biographies of the man (*Father Mychal Judge,* by Michael Ford and *The Book of Mychal,* by Michael Daly, among others) but also thanks to knowing several of his Franciscan brothers.

Or think of Henri Nouwen, the Dutch priest and psychologist whose perceptive books on the spiritual life, like the now-classic *The Return of the Prodigal Son,* were of inestimable help to millions of his readers. Toward the end of his life, he fell in love quite suddenly, and turbulently, with another man. How do I know that Father

Nouwen was gay? Again, based on not only biographies and essays (*Wounded Prophet,* by Michael Ford and *The Essential Henri Nouwen,* edited by Robert A. Jonas) but also, in this case, knowing the man with whom he fell in love.

Were these men saints? That's hard to say, but I'd argue that they were certainly holy, and therefore they can show us how one can be an LGBT person and holy.

When I mention this, some people profess surprise. But why are they surprised? Because they think gay people can't be holy? Some are offended. But why are they offended? Being gay is not a sin, and, from all accounts, Father Judge kept his vow of chastity and Father Nouwen his promise of celibacy.

Those who are surprised may be surprised to be greeted in heaven by more than a few gay and lesbian saints. And those who are offended may have their own offenses forgiven by those same saints.

Let's return to the concept of respect.

Respect also should be extended to the workplace, especially if that workplace is a church or church-related organization. To that end, I'm disheartened by the recent trend, in a few places, of the firing of LGBT people. According to New Ways Ministry, since 2010 almost seventy people in Catholic institutions in the United States have been fired, been forced to resign, had job offers rescinded, or had their jobs threatened because of their orientation—often after years of service in these positions and being known as LGBT people. This figure, according to New Ways, includes only those people whose situations have become public; anecdotally, many other instances are known.

Of course, church organizations have the authority to require their employees to follow church teachings. The problem is that this authority is applied in a highly *selective* way. Almost all the firings in recent years have focused on LGBT matters. Specifically, the firings have usually related to those employees who have entered into same-sex marriages, which is against church teaching, when one or the other partner has a public role in the church.

But if adherence to church teachings is going to be a litmus test for employment in Catholic institutions, then dioceses and parishes need to be consistent. Do we fire a straight man or woman who gets divorced and then remarries without an annulment? Divorce and remarriage of that sort are against church teaching. In fact, divorce is something Jesus himself forbade (Matt. 19:8–9). Do we fire women who bear children, or men who father children, out of wedlock? How about couples living together before being married? Do we give pink slips to people who practice birth control? All those actions are against church teaching too.

And what about church employees who are not Catholic? If we fire employees who do not agree with or adhere to church teaching, do we fire all Protestants who work in a Catholic institution because they do not believe in papal authority? That's an important church teaching. Do we fire Unitarians who do not believe in the Trinity? Do we fire all Jewish employees who do not believe in Jesus Christ, in the Incarnation or the Resurrection? Do we fire all agnostics and atheists who doubt or who do not believe in God?

Do we fire these people for such things? No, we do not. Why not? Because we are selective—perhaps unconsciously, perhaps consciously—about *which* church teachings matter.

Here is another way of looking at this kind of selectivity, one that shows us why it is especially problematic. Requiring church employees to adhere to church teachings means, at a more fundamental level, adhering to the Gospel. To be consistent, shouldn't we fire people for not helping the poor, for not being forgiving, or for not being loving? For being cruel?

That may sound odd, and it may even cause you to

roll your eyes, but why should it? These commands of Jesus are the most essential church teachings.

Some people have argued that those final categories are unenforceable because unlike entering into same-sex marriages, being cruel, for example, is not a "public sin," nor does it cause "public scandal." But anyone who has ever worked in any kind of professional setting—including a rectory, chancery, retreat house, hospital, or school—will tell you that being cruel is a very public act. And, to my mind, being a cruel person while working in a Catholic institution is indeed a "public scandal."

It is rather that we do not choose to focus on those things.

The selectivity of focus on LGBT matters when it comes to firings is, to use the words of the Catholic *Catechism,* a "sign of unjust discrimination" (No. 2358), something we are to avoid. Indeed, in 2016, *America* magazine published an editorial that said, "The high public profile of these firings, when combined with a lack of due process and the absence of any comparable policing of marital status for heterosexual employees, constitute signs of 'unjust discrimination' and the church in the United States should do more to avoid them."

One young gay man shared with me another perspective on this phenomenon. He wondered if the selectivity occurs not only because of homophobia but because straight men and women are never forced to consider what would happen if they were gay. Thus it is easier for them to condemn homosexuality because they see themselves as now and forever straight. "You can never be a hypocrite preaching about the 'sinful homosexual lifestyle,'" he wrote in an email, "because you will never find yourself where the temptation is present."

That was one reason he believed there was so much focus on this issue rather than other issues related to sexual morality—like premarital sex and divorce. Straight men and women might indeed engage in premarital sex or seek a divorce. But they are safe in condemning homosexuality because it will never be an experience they face. It is an interesting argument to consider.

# Compassion

What would it mean for the institutional church to show compassion to LGBT men and women?

The word *compassion* (from the Greek *paschō*) means "to experience with" or "to suffer with." So what would it mean for the institutional church not only to respect LGBT Catholics but also to be with them, to experience life with them, and even to suffer with them?

This question can be asked about the hierarchy as well as the entire church. It can be asked about bishops and priests as well as pastoral workers, directors of religious education, music ministers, teachers, administrators, and those who don't work in any official capacity in the church but who participate in the life of the church as faithful parishioners: Catholic men and women of all sorts. How can all of us experience and suffer with our LGBT brothers and sisters?

The first and most essential requirement is listening. It is impossible to experience a person's life, or to be compassionate, if you do not listen to the person or if you do not ask questions.

Questions that Catholic leaders might ask their LGBT brothers, sisters, and siblings are:

> *What was it like growing up as a gay boy, a lesbian girl, or a transgender person?*
>
> *What is your life like now?*
>
> *How have you suffered as a result of your orientation or gender identity?*
>
> *Where do you experience joy in your life?*
>
> *What is your experience of God?*
>
> *What is your experience of Jesus?*
>
> *What is your experience of the church?*
>
> *What do you hope for, long for, pray for?*

They might also ask the parents of LGBT Catholics these kinds of questions:

> *What is it like for you to have an LGBT child?*

*What was it like when your child shared his or her sexuality or identity with you?*

*What is your relationship with your child like now?*

*Do you yourself feel welcome in the church?*

*Do you ever fear that your child will leave the church? And if your child has left, how are you dealing with that?*

*How might the church be a more welcoming place for your child?*

*What is your own experience of God?*

*What do you hope for, long for, pray for—for both you and your child?*

For the church to exercise compassion, we need to listen. And when we listen, we will learn, we will be challenged, and we will be inspired.

Let me share six very brief stories that invite all of us to listen.

One of my oldest friends is a gay man named Mark, who was once a member of a Catholic religious order.

About twenty years ago, after Mark left the order, he came out as a gay man, and began living with his partner, to whom he is now legally married. His partner has a serious, long-term illness, and Mark has cared for him for many years, with great devotion and loving-kindness.

*What can we learn from Mark about love?*

An elderly man told me that his grandson recently came out to him as a gay man. I asked what he had said in response. He said that he had suspected for some time that his grandson was gay, and so when his grandson sat down to tell him, before a word was even on the young man's lips, the grandfather said, "I love you no matter what you're about to say."

*What can we learn from this grandfather about compassion?*

After a talk I gave at a Catholic college in Philadelphia, a young man told me that the first person to whom he came out as a gay man was a Catholic priest. During a high school retreat, he decided to publicly acknowledge his homosexuality, but he was so nervous that he was "literally shaking." The first thing the priest said to him was "Jesus loves you. And your church accepts you." The young man told me, "It saved my life."

*What can we learn from this priest about acceptance?*

A woman in her eighties, with snowy white hair and apple cheeks, came to my book-signing table after a talk I had given in Connecticut and said, "Father, I have something to tell you." The focus of the talk had been on Jesus, not on LGBT issues specifically. I thought she might share an insight about Jesus or tell me that she had been on a pilgrimage to the Holy Land. Instead she said, "Father, I have a grandchild who is transgender, and I love her so much. All I want is for her to feel welcome in the church."

*What can we learn from this grandmother about faith?*

At a parish in Boston, a gay man and a lesbian woman were invited to "respond" to my lecture on LGBT Catholics, in the spirit of fostering a real conversation. In her response, the lesbian woman, named Maggie, chose to discuss a reflection question that appears at the end of the book: "When you think about your sexual orientation or gender identity, what word do you use?" My intention was to invite readers to reflect on biblical passages about names and naming and encourage them to "name" their sexuality. So I had expected words like "gay," "lesbian," and "bisexual." But that night in the parish, Maggie said that when she read that question and thought of her sexuality, she thought of the word "joy." It was such a surprise!

*What can we learn from Maggie about sexuality?*

And perhaps the biggest surprise: On that same evening in Boston, a couple stayed afterward to have their book signed. One was a transgender woman—that is, a woman who had begun her life as a man. The other was a "cisgender woman"—that is, someone born a woman who is still a woman. (As I've noted previously, I have tried to be mindful of contemporary terminology, though I recognize that these terms get dated quickly.)

The cisgender woman told me that the two had been married for many years, which confused me, since same-sex marriage had not been legal for that long in Massachusetts. She sensed my confusion, smiled, and said, "I married her when she was still a man."

I was reduced to stunned silence. Here was an apparently straight woman who had married a straight man who was now a woman. How had she done it? "Love is love," she said.

Here is a marriage that almost every church official would probably consider "irregular," to use the official ecclesiastical term. Yet it was a model of faithfulness. Even after one partner had "transitioned," the marriage was still intact.

*What can we learn from them about fidelity?*

For any learning to happen, we need to listen.

When we listen carefully, we will also hear the calls for help and prayer, especially in times and places of persecution. And when our LGBT brothers and sisters and siblings are persecuted, church leaders are called to stand with them. In many parts of the world, LGBT persons are liable to experience appalling incidents of prejudice, violence, and even murder. "Roundups" of LGBT people happen regularly in countries like Indonesia, Egypt, Azerbaijan, and Chechnya. In some countries, a person can be jailed or even *executed* for being gay or having same-sex relations. As of this writing, engaging in same-sex relations is a crime in over seventy countries, and simply being gay or bisexual is punishable by death in thirteen countries.

In these countries, the institutional church has an absolute moral duty to stand up for our brothers and sisters, publicly. Sadly, this does not happen very often, and in fact, a few church leaders have supported some of these discriminatory laws. But embedded in Catholic teaching is a call to stand with our LGBT brothers and sisters. The *Catechism* says "every sign of unjust discrimination" must be avoided (No. 2358). More fundamentally, helping, defending, and caring for someone who is being beaten is surely part of compassion. It is part of being a disciple of Jesus Christ. If you doubt that, consider the Parable of the Good Samaritan (Lk. 10:25–37).

Closer to home, what would it mean for the church in the United States to say, when needed, "It is wrong to treat the LGBT community like this"? Catholic leaders regularly publish statements—as they should—defending the unborn, refugees and migrants, the poor, the homeless, the aged. This is one way to stand with people: by putting yourself out there, even taking heat for them.

But where are statements specifically in support of our LGBT brothers, sisters, and siblings? When I ask this, some people say, "You can't compare what refugees face with what LGBT people face." As someone who worked with refugees in East Africa for two years, I know that's often the case. But it is also important not to ignore the disproportionately high rates of suicide among LGBT youths and the fact that LGBT people are the victims of proportionally more hate crimes than any other minority group in this country.

Here are some statistics from The Trevor Project, an organization that helps prevent teen LGBT suicides, which remind us that these are "life issues."

- Lesbian, gay, and bisexual youth are almost *five times* as likely to have attempted suicide compared to straight youth.

- Lesbian, gay, and bisexual youth seriously contemplate suicide at almost *three times* the rate of straight youth.

- Lesbian, gay, and bisexual youth who come from "highly rejecting" families are *8.4 times* as likely to have attempted suicide as LGBT peers who have reported no or low levels of family rejection.

- In a national study, *forty percent* of transgender adults reported having made a suicide attempt, and *ninety-two percent* of these individuals reported having attempted suicide before age twenty-five.

- Every instance of victimization of lesbian, gay, and bisexual youth, such as physical harassment, or verbal harassment or abuse, increases the likelihood of self-harming behavior by *2.5 times* on the average.

The bullying of LGBT students in schools is also an evil that should be squarely opposed, particularly given the Catholic Church's long history and extensive experience with running elementary, middle, and high schools.

GLSEN, a group that advocates for the protection of LGBT students in the United States, reports these sobering statistics about middle school and high school students who are LGBT:

- *Eighty-five percent* report being verbally harassed.

- *Sixty-three percent* report hearing homophobic remarks from teachers or the school staff.

- *Fifty-seven percent* feel unsafe because of their sexual orientations.

- *Fifty-seven percent* did not report experiences of bullying because they doubted that an intervention would occur.

- *Sixty-three percent* who did report bullying said that the school did nothing or told them to ignore it.

As I've mentioned before, in the wake of the massacre at a gay nightclub in Orlando in 2016, when the LGBT community across the country was grieving, I was discouraged that more bishops did not immediately signal their support. Some did. But imagine if the attacks had been on, God forbid, a Methodist church. Many bishops would have said, "We stand with our Methodist brothers and sisters." Why didn't more Catholic leaders name our LGBT brothers and sisters in Orlando? To me, it seemed a failure of compassion, a failure to experience with, and a failure to suffer with. Orlando invites us all to reflect on this.

Orlando also invites us to reflect on the implications of these failures. As James F. Keenan, SJ, professor of moral theology at Boston College, regularly pointed out to our class in graduate school, more often than not, Jesus did not critique people who were weak but trying. Rather, the gospels show that Jesus critiqued people who were strong but not bothering. For example, the rich man who doesn't bother to help the poor man by his door (Lk. 16:19–31), the religious leader who doesn't bother to consider that someone needs healing on a Sabbath (Lk. 13:10–16), and the Pharisee who doesn't bother to offer Jesus a welcome (Lk. 7:36–45).

For Jesus, sin was, as Father Keenan said, "a failure to bother to love." After Orlando, I think, many in the church failed to bother to love. How often do all of us fail to bother in this way?

We need not look far for a model for how to proceed. God did this for all of us—in Jesus. The opening lines of the Gospel of John tell us, "The Word became flesh and lived among us" (Jn. 1:14). A more accurate rendering of the Greek is: "The Word became flesh and pitched its tent among us" (*eskēnōsen en hēmin*). Isn't that a beautiful phrase? God pitched his tent with us. God entered our world to live among us. This is what Jesus did. He lived alongside us, took our side, even died like us.

This is what the church is called to do with all marginalized groups, as Pope Francis has often reminded us, including LGBT Catholics: to experience their lives and suffer with them. "For Jesus," said Francis in a homily in 2015 to a group of newly named cardinals, "what matters above all is reaching out to save those far off, healing the wounds of the sick, restoring everyone to God's family! And this is scandalous to some people!"

So we need to experience life with LGBT people. To enter into their sufferings. And to enter into their joys as well! Because Jesus came to experience all parts of our lives, not just the sorrowful parts. LGBT people, though they may suffer persecution, share in the joys of the human condition.

Can you rejoice with our LGBT brothers and sisters? Can the entire church—from popes to bishops to priests to pastoral associates to parishioners—rejoice in the gifts and talents, the joys and hopes, the enthusiasm and energy, brought by LGBT Catholics?

Especially among younger LGBT people, I find a tremendous zest for the faith. Perhaps this is because, unlike their older brothers and sisters, they have grown up in a society where they feel more comfortable about their sexuality, and so they may feel less burdened by their sexual identity. (This is just my own supposition.) Over-all, younger LGBT people who are active in the church bring a great many gifts, which we can celebrate and treasure.

We can celebrate and treasure more than simply the gifts of LGBT Catholics. We can celebrate and treasure *them*. This is a kind of compassion too—to share in their whole lives and to experience the Christian joy that LGBT men and women, young and old, bring to the church.

# Sensitivity

How can the institutional church be *sensitive* toward LGBT people? That's a beautiful word used by the *Catechism*.

My old *Merriam-Webster's Dictionary* defines *sensitivity* as an "awareness or understanding of the feelings of other people." That's related to Pope Francis's call for the church to be a church of "encounter" and "accompaniment."

To begin with, it is nearly impossible to know another person's feelings at a distance. You cannot understand the feelings of a community if you don't *know* the community. You can't be sensitive to the LGBT community if you only issue documents about them, preach about them, or tweet about them, without knowing them.

One reason the institutional church has struggled with sensitivity is that, based on my observations, many church leaders still do not know many gay and lesbian people. The temptation is to smile and say that church leaders do know people who are gay: priests and members of religious orders who are not public about their sexual orientation. But my point is a larger one. Many church leaders do not know, on a personal level, LGBT people who are public about their sexuality and identity. That lack of familiarity and friendship means it is more difficult to be sensitive. How can you be sensitive to people's situations if you don't know them? One invitation for the hierarchy, then, is to come to know LGBT Catholics as friends.

Some of the reasons behind this lack of familiarity and friendship are easy to understand. A friend of mine, a gay man named Brian, once worked on the staff of a U.S. bishop. Often they would share car rides together— traveling to a diocesan meeting or visiting a parish. While driving, the bishop would often make homophobic comments that deeply offended my friend, who was working hard in the bishop's office, specifically on issues of social justice. In fact, the bishop often praised him on his work ethic. (Later, Brian would work in a similar capacity in the office of the U.S. Conference of Catholic Bishops.)

So, I once asked Brian why he didn't come out to his boss. "Are you kidding?" he said. "He's the last person I would come out to. He's very homophobic, and I'm worried I could lose my job." So the bishop was working with a person he admired and relied upon and who, unbeknownst to him, was also gay. His homophobia had made it more difficult for LGBT people to feel comfortable around him, and perhaps as a result, his homophobia continued unabated.

In 2015, Cardinal Christoph Schönborn, the archbishop of Vienna, reminded the church of the importance of familiarity and friendship at the meeting of the Synod of Bishops on the Family, the gathering of Catholic bishops who assembled at the invitation of Pope Francis to discuss a wide variety of issues related to the family, and as it turned out, human sexuality. Cardinal Schönborn spoke of a gay couple he knew who had transformed his understanding of LGBT people. He even offered some qualified praise for his friend's same-sex union. The cardinal said:

> One shares one's life, one shares the joys and sufferings, one helps one another. We must recognize that this person has made an important step for his own good and for the good of others, even though, of course, this is not a situation that the church can consider regular.

He also overruled a priest in his archdiocese who had prohibited a man in a same-sex union from serving on a parish council. That is, Cardinal Schönborn stood with his LGBT brother. Two years later, while speaking about the church's support of family life in general, he said, "Favoring the family does not mean disfavoring other forms of life—even those living in a same-sex partnership need their families." Much of his sensitivity came from his experience of, knowledge of, and friendship with LGBT people.

Cardinal Schönborn said of the church, "It must accompany people."

In this, as in all things, Jesus is our model. When Jesus encountered people on the margins, he saw not categories but individuals. To be clear, I am not saying that LGBT people should be, or should feel, marginalized. Rather, I am saying that within the church many of them do find themselves marginalized. They are seen as "other."

But for Jesus there was no "other." Jesus saw beyond categories; he met people where they were and accompanied them.

The Gospel of Matthew, for example, tells the story of Jesus meeting a Roman centurion in Capernaum, a fishing town on the Sea of Galilee (Matt. 8:5–13). The centurion approaches Jesus to ask for healing for his servant. When Jesus offers to come to the centurion's house, the man says, "Lord, I am not worthy to have you come under my roof." The centurion tells Jesus that he knows something about authority, as he too has men under his command. All Jesus needs to do, he says, is to give the word. Jesus professes amazement at the centurion's faith and heals his servant.

In other words, although the centurion was not Jewish and therefore lived on the margins of that social milieu, Jesus saw someone in need, listened to his story, and responded to his need.

In another story, in Luke's Gospel, Jesus is passing through Jericho with his disciples when he encounters a man named Zacchaeus, the chief tax collector in this large town (Lk. 19:1–10). In that story, Zacchaeus, who is described as "short in stature," climbs a sycamore tree because "he was trying to see who Jesus was." He is prevented from seeing Jesus "on account of the crowd."

When Jesus sees Zacchaeus perched in the tree, he sees a person seeking to encounter him. Here it's important to note that Zacchaeus was the chief tax collector in the region, and therefore would also have been considered the "chief sinner" in that society. Again, he is someone on the margins. Nonetheless, Jesus calls to Zacchaeus in the tree and invites himself to the man's house.

Jesus was willing to be with, stand with, and befriend all these people who would have felt themselves as either on the margins or outside the margins of first-century Jewish society in Galilee and Judea.

In his ministry to those on the margins, the movement for Jesus was always from the outside in. He brought those on the outside in. At the same time, he brought his disciples, and those who were on the inside, out. He moved them out toward the margins.

Jesus's message was one of inclusion, communicated through speaking to people, healing them, or offering them what biblical scholars call "table fellowship"—that is, dining with them, a sign of welcome and acceptance in first-century Palestine. He did this again and again, with not only the Roman centurion and Zacchaeus but other tax collectors, as well as prostitutes, a Samaritan woman, and many of the sick, who also would have been viewed as outcasts.

My point is not that LGBT people should be treated as sinners, as many of these people were considered in those days—*for we are all sinners.* Rather, it is that Jesus continually reached out to all those who felt marginalized in any way.

In fact, Jesus was often criticized for this practice. But Jesus's movement was about inclusion. He was creating a sense of "us."

For with Jesus, there is no us and them. There is only us.

One common objection here is to say, "No, Jesus always told them, first of all, not to sin!" We cannot meet LGBT people because they are sinning, goes the argument, and when we do meet them, the first thing we must say is "Stop sinning!"

But more often than not, this is not Jesus's way.

In the story of the Roman centurion, for example, Jesus encounters not only someone who is not Jewish but a man who likely believes in multiple gods. But Jesus doesn't shout "Pagan!" or scold him for not being Jewish. Instead, he professes astonishment at the man's faith, which he declares greater than he has found anywhere in Israel, and then he heals his servant.

Indeed, Luke's Gospel tells us explicitly that Jesus was "amazed" by the centurion's faith. In other words, Jesus was open to being surprised by something about a person on the margins.

Likewise, in the story of Zacchaeus, after spying the tax collector perched in the tree, a man who simply wants to see "who Jesus was," he doesn't point to him and shout "Sinner!" Instead Jesus says that he will go to Zacchaeus's house, a public sign of welcome, before Zacchaeus has said or done anything. Only *after* Jesus offers him welcome is Zacchaeus moved to conversion, promising to pay back anyone he might have defrauded.

Even in Jesus's time this provoked opposition. The crowd, says Luke's Gospel, "began to grumble" at Jesus's offer of welcome to Zacchaeus. As the crowd often does today!

But for Jesus it is most often *community first*—meeting, encountering, including—*and conversion second.*

Here again I am talking about the conversion that all of us need, not simply LGBT people. We are all called to *metanoia,* a conversion of hearts and minds.

In fact, in a fascinating reflection on Jesus's interactions with tax collectors in the Gospel of Mark—in the *Sacra Pagina* series of bible commentaries—two distinguished New Testament scholars, Daniel J. Harrington, SJ, and John R. Donahue, SJ, underline an important aspect of such stories. Except for Matthew (or Levi), the tax collector who leaves his job to follow Jesus, "there is no indication that the toll collectors abandoned their profession after contact with Jesus."

The same holds true for Zacchaeus in Luke's Gospel: the man has undergone a *metanoia,* but there is no indication that he ceased being a tax collector. And, of course, Jesus continued to meet and dine with this group of marginal people, which caused intense controversy (Mk 2: 13-17).

In that case, that is, what is Jesus's point?

According to Fathers Harrington and Donahue, "it

amounted to a simple message that God loved these people and that they would be part of the kingdom being
inaugurated by Jesus."

They conclude their analysis with this observation:

> The practice of Jesus depicted here manifests a prefer-
> ence for the marginal. . . . Churches today are chal-
> lenged to expend their energy and resources not only
> on the "well" and the strong but also (and especially)
> on those who need healing and a sense of divine
> acceptance.

Pope Francis echoed this approach during an in-flight
press conference in 2016, on his return to Rome from
the countries of Georgia and Azerbaijan. "People must
be accompanied, as Jesus accompanied them," he said.
"When a person who has this situation comes before
Jesus, Jesus will surely not say: 'Go away because you're
homosexual.'"

Sensitivity is based on encounter, accompaniment,
and friendship.

❧ ❧

Where does this lead? To the second meaning of *sensitivity*, which is, in common parlance, a heightened aware-

ness of what might hurt or offend someone. When we are sensitive to people's situations, we are sensitive to anything that might needlessly offend.

One way to be sensitive is to consider the language we use. Some bishops have recently called for the church to revisit the phrase "objectively disordered" when it comes to describing the homosexual inclination (as it is in the *Catechism,* No. 2358). The phrase relates to the orientation, not the person, but it is still, as countless LGBT people have told me, needlessly hurtful to them.

To understand more of the context of that phrase, here is the *Catechism*'s entire teaching on the matter, and on homosexuality in general:

2357 Homosexuality refers to relations between men or between women who experience an exclusive or predominant sexual attraction toward persons of the same sex. It has taken a great variety of forms through the centuries and in different cultures. Its psychological genesis remains largely unexplained. Basing itself on Sacred Scripture, which presents homosexual acts as acts of grave depravity, tradition has always declared that "homosexual acts are intrinsically disordered." They are contrary to the natural law. They close the sexual act to the gift of life. They do not proceed from a genuine affective and sexual complementarity. Under no circumstances can they be approved.

**2358** The number of men and women who have deep-seated homosexual tendencies is not negligible. This inclination, which is objectively disordered, constitutes for most of them a trial. They must be accepted with respect, compassion, and sensitivity. Every sign of unjust discrimination in their regard should be avoided. These persons are called to fulfill God's will in their lives and, if they are Christians, to unite to the sacrifice of the Lord's Cross the difficulties they may encounter from their condition.

**2359** Homosexual persons are called to chastity. By the virtues of self-mastery that teach them inner freedom, at times by the support of disinterested friendship, by prayer and sacramental grace, they can and should gradually and resolutely approach Christian perfection.

Our sexuality, in a sense, touches everything we do, including the way we love, even when the sexual expression of that love is neither involved nor even contemplated. So to call a person's sexuality "objectively disordered" is to tell a person that all of his or her love, even the most chaste, is disordered. For many LGBT Catholics, that seems unnecessarily cruel.

Revising, updating, or even setting aside such language was discussed at the Synod on the Family, according to several news outlets. Later, in 2016, an Australian bishop, Vincent Long Van Nguyen, said in a lecture:

> We cannot talk about the integrity of creation, the universal and inclusive love of God, while at the same time colluding with the forces of oppression in the ill-treatment of racial minorities, women, and homosexual persons. . . . It won't wash with young people, especially when we purport to treat gay people with love and compassion and yet define their sexuality as "intrinsically disordered."

After a parish talk, the mother of a gay son asked me, "Do people understand what it could mean for a fourteen-year-old gay boy to read language like that? It could *destroy* him."

Part of sensitivity is understanding this. Part of sensitivity is listening to this mother.

# Respect

Now let's take a walk on the other lane on the bridge, the one that leads from the LGBT community to the institutional church. What would it mean for LGBT Catholics to treat the institutional church with respect, compassion, and sensitivity?

In the Catholic Church, the hierarchy possesses immense institutional power. Members of the hierarchy have the power to allow individuals to receive the sacraments, to permit or prevent priests from celebrating the sacraments, to open or close diocesan or parish ministries, to allow people to retain their jobs in Catholic institutions, and so on.

But LGBT Catholics have power as well. Increasingly, for instance, the Western media has been more sympathetic to the LGBT community than to the Catholic hierarchy. That's a kind of "soft power." Still, in the institutional church, it is the hierarchy that operates from the position of power.

LGBT Catholics are called to treat those people in power with respect, compassion, and sensitivity. Why? Because, as I mentioned, it's a two-way bridge. More important, LGBT Catholics are Christians, and those virtues express Christian love. Those virtues also help to build up the entire community.

For many LGBT Catholics this may be a challenge or even painful to hear, given how they have been treated over the years. I only invite them to meditate on what the words *respect, compassion,* and *sensitivity* mean when applied to their relationship with the church. This is the moment to set aside the us-and-them mentality, for there is no us and them in the church.

What would it mean for the LGBT community to show respect to the church? Here I am speaking specifically about the pope and the bishops—that is, the hierarchy and, more broadly, the magisterium, the teaching authority of the church.

Catholics believe that bishops, priests, and deacons receive at their ordinations the grace for a special ministry of leadership in the church. We also believe that bishops have an authority that comes down to them from the apostles. This is what we mean, in part, when we profess our belief each Sunday at Mass that the church is "apostolic." Also, we believe that the Holy Spirit inspires and guides the church. Certainly this happens through the People of God, who, as the Second Vatican Council taught, are imbued with the Spirit, but it also happens through popes, bishops, and clergy by virtue of their ordination and their offices.

The institutional church—popes and councils, archbishops and bishops—speak with authority in their role as teachers. They don't all speak with the same level of authority (more about that later), but Catholics must prayerfully consider what they are teaching. To do that, we are called to listen. Their teaching deserves our respect.

So, first, we are called to listen. On all matters, not just LGBT issues, the episcopacy speaks with authority and draws from a great well of tradition. When bishops speak on matters like—but not confined to—love, forgiveness, and mercy, as well as caring for the poor, the marginalized, the unborn, the homeless, prisoners, refugees, and so on, they are drawing from not only the Gospels but also the spiritual treasury of the church's tradition. Often, especially on social justice issues, bishops will challenge us with a wisdom that we may hear nowhere else in the world.

When the episcopacy speaks about LGBT matters in a way that LGBT Catholics don't agree with or that angers or even offends them, LGBT Catholics are invited to challenge themselves to listen closely. Ask: "What are they saying? Why are they saying it? What lies behind their words?" LGBT Catholics are called to listen, consider, pray, and of course use their informed consciences as they discern how to lead their lives.

Beyond what one might call ecclesial respect, the hierarchy deserves simple human respect. Often I'm saddened by the things I hear some LGBT Catholics and their allies say about certain bishops. I hear these things privately but also publicly. Recently one LGBT group, in response to a statement from bishops on same-sex marriage, said that the bishops should stop being "locked in their ivory towers." I thought, *Really? You're saying that to bishops in poor dioceses too? That they live in "ivory towers"? To bishops who minister to the poor, oversee parishes in inner-city neighborhoods, sponsor schools that educate children of poor families, and manage Catholic Charities offices?* You may disagree with the bishops, but that kind of language is not only disrespectful; it's inaccurate.

More seriously, LGBT Catholics and their allies sometimes mock bishops for their promises of celibacy, their residences, and especially the clothes they wear. The barely disguised implication of posting online photos of bishops wearing elaborate liturgical vestments is that they are effeminate, they are hypocrites, or they are repressed gay men.

Does the LGBT community want to proceed in this way? Do gay men want to mock bishops as effeminate when many gay men were most likely teased about precisely that when they were young? Is this not simply perpetuating a cycle of hatred? How can people castigate a bishop for not respecting the LGBT community when they do not afford him respect in the process? Is it right for people to critique others for their supposed un-Christian attitudes by themselves being un-Christian?

Some LGBT people think this is a justifiable condemnation of what they see as hypocrisy. One gay man told me that he felt it was not only justifiable but "therapeutic," particularly when it was directed against church leaders who had, in his words, "said some awful stuff about gays."

But I invite LGBT people to think about this question: Is this in keeping with our Christian call? To me, it seems a perpetuation of a cycle of hatred.

This may be very hard for people who feel beaten down by the church to hear. One gay friend recently told me that this mockery comes not from a place of hatred but from a sense of betrayal. "Knowing that there are some gay members in the hierarchy," he wrote to me recently, "it is both frustrating and heartbreaking to hear them preach down to LGBT laypeople."

But being respectful of people with whom you disagree is at the heart of the Christian way. And part of this is surely about forgiveness, an essential Christian virtue.

Even from a human point of view, it's good strategy. If you sincerely want to influence the church's perspective on LGBT matters, it helps to earn the trust of members of the hierarchy. One way to do that is by respecting them. Again, this may be very difficult for LGBT people to hear. But most church officials, at least the ones I know, simply respond better to gentle conversation than to angry protests. In fact, that may be true not only for most bishops but for most people. So both the Christian approach and simple human wisdom would say, "Respect them."

To that end, a story: After I had given a talk at the Catholic center at a large university, the father of a gay man stood up to ask a question. The father told me that he and his wife had welcomed their son with open arms and a loving heart after he shared his sexuality with them. At the same time, the father told the crowd, their local bishop had not been welcoming to LGBT people. And the father told me a remarkable story—hopeful but not sugarcoated—about bridge building with respect. What follows is the story in his own words, from a later letter he sent me, only slightly edited.

Not long ago, our new bishop was presiding at his first confirmation, which was celebrated at our parish. During his homily, he preached about the evils of same-sex marriage. This became part of his standard homily at confirmations, which came after Pope Francis had stated that the church had become "obsessed" with homosexuality and needed to find a "new balance" in preaching.

I wrote the bishop a somewhat angry letter, contrasting the pope's message with his. I received a somewhat angry letter back. Then I wrote him a slightly less angry letter, and he wrote me a slightly less angry letter back. I did not pursue further communication.

A turning point came while I was reading the *Rule of Saint Benedict,* the sixth-century text that governs life in Benedictine communities. I'm a "Lay Cistercian," which means that I'm a layperson affiliated with a nearby abbey, and we make a commitment to live life under the *Rule,* as adapted to our own individual lives.

At one point, Saint Benedict writes: "Bear injuries patiently. Love your enemies (Matt. 5:44; Lk. 6:27). If people curse you, do not curse them back but bless them instead."

These words struck me in the heart. In my mind, I had created an enemy in the bishop. For the first time, I had to live the hardest words in the Bible: "Love your enemies." I prayed for him and for my anger.

At this point, I remembered something important. A few years ago, my wife and I attended a conference at our parish called "Welcoming Gay Catholics to the Church," where we learned about the *Catechism*'s teaching that gay folks should be treated with "respect, compassion, and sensitivity."

After I had the realization about the bishop, I said to my wife, "I should treat the bishop with the same respect, compassion, and sensitivity that I want him to treat our son with. I have to be the alternative I want him to be."

So I wrote a new letter, in the spirit of Saint Benedict, citing the high LGBT suicide rates and presenting it as a "life issue," and asked if we could discuss this out of a spirit of love for my son and love for our church.

To my surprise, his secretary called to set up an

appointment. At our first meeting, we spoke for an hour and a half. I made it as personal as I could, by sharing my story about my wife and our son (I brought pictures, from when he was little to his time as an Eagle Scout to a grown man), how our son came out to us, and how I suspected that he might be gay since he was three years old.

For my part, I attempted to appeal to his heart and not just engage in an intellectual debate.

Then I said, "The most painful part of this journey for my son, my wife, and me has been his experience of unwelcome, and even rejection, by the church."

At this point the bishop asked with a genuinely puzzled look, "May I ask why he feels that way?"

The first thought that ran through my mind was "You've got to be kidding me!"

Then I realized that he had probably never had a conversation like this with the parent of a gay child. Although I was disappointed that he would not be aware of how my son or any LGBT person would feel, I appreciated that he was open, honest, and seeking to understand. His question made me realize the importance of our meeting if there is to be any hope of movement on this issue in our church.

During our discussion, I quoted often from *Al-*

*ways Our Children,* the United States Conference of
Catholic Bishops' document on ministry to LGBT
people from 1997. At the end of our first session,
he said, "You've quoted *Always Our Children,* but
are you aware of the updated 2006 document?" I
was not. Again, to my surprise, he invited me back
to comment on the 2006 document and the group
called Courage, which encourages LGBT people
to live chastity. I read, researched, and prayed over
the 2006 document, which was difficult for me, and
we met to discuss it, for over an hour. Then we met
again to discuss Courage, again for over an hour. I
am supposed to be meeting with him again in a few
months.

I'm not sure how much headway is being made,
but my hope and prayer is that something has happened, and I will leave that to the Holy Spirit. As
much as I disagree with his theology and what I saw
as his clinging to natural law over science and scripture, I admire the bishop for his willingness to meet
with me and for being so generous with his time.

In my experience, this is the kind of bridge building that will ultimately bear the most fruit. There is a
time for protest, but there is also a time for respectful
dialogue.

# Compassion

What would it mean to show compassion to the hierarchy?

First, let's recall the definition of *compassion*: "to experience with" or "to suffer with." Part of this, as I mentioned, is knowing what a person's life is like. Part of compassion toward the institutional church, then, is a real understanding of the lives of people in power.

In my life as a Jesuit, I have met many cardinals, archbishops, and bishops. Quite a few I consider friends and many have been very kind to me personally. All the ones I've met are hardworking and prayerful men, loyal servants of the church who try to carry out the ministries for which they were ordained.

A few years ago, for example, one cardinal met a friend of mine whose mother had a life-threatening illness. Though we were all together at a crowded event, the cardinal took my friend aside, spoke with him privately, prayed with him on the spot, and then asked for his mother's phone number. The next day, the cardinal called her at home and found out she was unavailable. "When would be a good time to call back?" he asked. Fifteen minutes later, he called and spoke to her at length, easing her worries and fears.

Another cardinal surprised me by calling one night to encourage me to continue my ministry to LGBT people and shared with me his own efforts at outreach to that community. "Keep it up!" he said.

An archbishop became a friend after he invited me to speak to a gathering in his archdiocese. After hosting me for a relaxed meal with members of his staff the night before, he picked me up at 5:30 the next morning in his little car and drove me for an hour to the church where the lecture was to be held. During the ride, he shared, with great transparency, the joys and frustrations of his ministry.

And one bishop who works in the Vatican, with whom I've become friends and who offers me advice on any number of topics, likes to tell me lighthearted stories about how his mother is not impressed by his being a bishop, nor by what she calls his "funny hat."

I recount these stories not to show how many cardinals and bishops I know but to remind readers that members of the hierarchy are more than what people may read or hear about them. The same goes for all church leaders, clergy and lay. Inasmuch as the institutional church is invited to come to know LGBT people as their brothers and sisters, the LGBT community is invited to come to know these church leaders as their brothers.

Seeing them as people who are trying their best to love is part of compassion. So is understanding the responsibilities of their jobs.

These days, in addition to the normal "triple ministry" of bishops to "teach, govern, and sanctify" (that is, teach the Gospel, manage the diocese, and celebrate the sacraments), bishops have to do the following:

*Staff parishes in the face of rapidly declining vocations to the priesthood and religious orders;*

*Deal with the fallout—financial, legal, and emotional— from clergy sex-abuse cases, usually cases they had nothing to do with;*

*Decide which parishes and schools to close or consolidate in the face of emotional pleas and angry protests from parishioners, neighbors, students, and alumni;*

*Help raise money for nearly every institution in their diocese, including schools, hospitals, retreat houses, retirement communities for priests, and social service agencies;*

*In some cases deal with a growing diocese and increased numbers of parishioners in the face of a lack of resources and infrastructure; and*

*Answer complaints from furious Catholics, which pour into their chanceries about everything you can imagine, including supposed liturgical abuses during Mass, stray comments a priest made in a homily, an article they didn't like in the diocesan newspaper, even the fact that a Catholic received an award from a group they don't like.*

Not seeing these church leaders in the context of their complicated duties is to miss the truth of the situation; it may also signal a lack of compassion, which hampers receptivity of the message being communicated. There was a kind of compassion, for example, shown by the father of the gay man in the previous chapter, who tried to understand the bishop as someone who had perhaps never before met the parent of a gay child.

Compassion also leads us to what might be called an "equality of heart." This means coming to see that at least a few people in positions of leadership in the church may themselves be struggling. They might be homosexual men who at a younger age were tortured by the same hateful attitudes most LGBT people experienced growing up and who entered a religious world that seemed to afford them some safety and privacy.

The Irish novelist Colm Tóibín, who is openly gay, writing in the *London Review of Books* in 2010, offered a perceptive and sympathetic summary of what this might have been like. He recalled attending a workshop, at age sixteen, for boys who believed they had a vocation to the priesthood:

> Some of the reasons why gay men became priests are obvious and simple; others are not. Becoming a priest, first of all, seemed to solve the problem of not wanting others to know that you were queer. As a priest, you could be celibate or unmarried, and everyone would understand the reasons. It was because you had a vocation; you had been called by God, had been specially chosen by him. For other boys, the idea of never having sex with a woman was something they could not even entertain. For you, such sex was problematic; thus you had no blueprint for an easy future. The prospect, on the other hand, of making a vow in holiness never to have sex with a

woman offered you relief. The idea that you might want to have sex with men, that you might be "that way inclined," as they used to say, was not even mentioned, not once, during that workshop in which everything under the sun was discussed.

These are far from the only reasons that some gay men enter diocesan seminaries and religious houses of formation. In general, gay priests and members of religious orders enter for the same reasons their straight counterparts do: they feel called by God to follow the Gospel in this way, to serve the church in this way, to help people in this way. Still, the reasons adduced by Mr. Tóibín may have been additional factors in the particular appeal of that life: a certain privacy, a way to serve God without having to admit one's sexuality. A few may have remained with that worldview even as, over the last few decades, the truth about being gay gradually became more easily understood and less terrifying to live with.

This is what it is like to have been burdened by the effects of the hatred of gays and lesbians, particularly the deep-seated hatred that existed decades ago, and not being able to admit to a very private part of oneself. So LGBT Catholics are invited to feel for and pray for those whom the theologian James Alison describes as our "struggling brothers," even when their own backgrounds sometimes lead them to behave as if they were the enemies of the LGBT community.

The invitation is to see these bishops and other church leaders in their humanity, in their complexity, and amid the burdens of their ministries. I know this may be a very difficult task for some LGBT people, and also that church leaders are likewise called to understand the complexities of LGBT lives, but there is Christian compassion in trying to do this.

Many LGBT people feel that the members of the institutional church, or at least a few bishops and priests, have persecuted them. They see these men as their enemies, their persecutors, or, at the very least, as men who misunderstand them. And sadly, some bishops, priests, and deacons have indeed said and done ignorant, hurtful, and even hateful things.

One gay friend of mine said that he was particularly angry in the wake of the clergy sex-abuse crisis. After years of trying to stay with the church, despite feeling unwelcome, he felt deeply betrayed by the institution. "I was furious," he told me. How could he accept condemnations of his own sexuality from members of the hierarchy who had covered up the crime of sex abuse?

This should not be a surprising statement. Catholics— straight and LGBT—were rightly outraged over the sex-abuse crisis, reports of which peaked in the early 2000s.

The sexual abuse perpetrated on young children by priests and religious brothers (and occasionally sisters) were appalling crimes, and in response, many Catholics walked away from their church. For some LGBT people, as my friend's comments echoed, discovering that some members of the same hierarchy who had condemned them as "objectively disordered" had either mishandled or turned a blind eye to clergy abuse of children was simply too much to stand.

In my years of counseling and speaking with LGBT men and women, I have also heard countless stories of cruel and heartless comments made by priests in homilies or in private conversations that betray the most hateful attitudes toward LGBT people. Over and over, I would hear the same question: "How can I stay in a church that treats me like this?" But I believe that these actions represent a minority in the hierarchy and in the clergy, albeit one that until recently seemed to hold some sway in the church; that the tide is slowly changing; and that Pope Francis's papacy and the actions of a number of church leaders today are helping to heal some of that hurt. Many church leaders—bishops and priests—manifest a deep understanding of the hurt LGBT Catholics have felt.

In the wake of the shootings at the Pulse nightclub in Orlando, for example, Bishop Robert Lynch, of Saint

Petersburg, Florida, who has since retired, wrote this on his blog:

> Sadly, it is religion, including our own, which targets, mostly verbally, and also often breeds contempt for gays, lesbians, and transgender people. Attacks today on LGBT men and women often plant the seed of contempt, then hatred, which can ultimately lead to violence. Those women and men who were mowed down early yesterday morning were all made in the image and likeness of God. We teach that. We should believe that. We must stand for that. Without yet knowing who perpetrated the Pulse mass murders, when I saw the Imam come forward at a press conference yesterday morning, I knew that somewhere in the story there would be a search to find religious roots. While deranged people do senseless things, all of us observe, judge, and act from some kind of religious background. Singling out people for victimization because of their religion, their sexual orientation, their nationality, must be offensive to God's ears. It has to stop also.

In other words, many Catholic leaders do stand with the LGBT community. And the church is changing with respect to its welcome.

One of the most extraordinary signs of this recent change was the public welcome of a group of LGBT pilgrims by Cardinal Joseph Tobin, the archbishop of Newark.

A group called In God's Image, which works with fifteen parishes in New Jersey, Pennsylvania, and New York, gathers together LGBT people for reflection and faith sharing. In 2017, the group had an idea to organize a pilgrimage for LGBT Catholics to the Cathedral Basilica of the Sacred Heart in Newark. When contacted, Cardinal Tobin surprised them with a letter, saying, "I am delighted that you and the LGBTQ brothers and sisters plan to visit our beautiful cathedral."

On the day of the pilgrimage, over one hundred fifty LGBT pilgrims journeyed to the magnificent cathedral, where Mass was celebrated by a bishop, along with several priests as concelebrants. Beforehand, Cardinal Tobin, resplendent in a bright red cassock, stood before the ornate main altar and welcomed the pilgrims with words from the Old Testament. "I am Joseph, your brother," he said. "I am your brother, as a disciple of Jesus. I am your brother, as a sinner who finds mercy with the Lord."

In a front-page story in the *New York Times,* Cardinal Tobin explained, "The word I use is 'welcome' . . . These are people that have not felt welcome in other places. My prayer for them is that they do. Today in the Catholic Church, we read a passage that says you have to be able to give a reason for your hope. And I'm praying that this pilgrimage for them, and really for the whole church, is a reason for hope."

So increasing numbers of bishops are welcoming.

Incidentally, I recently gave a talk at one of the parishes whose LGBT lay leaders had helped to arrange the pilgrimage in Newark. In front of the church was something that surprised and moved me: a stone memorial in a small garden a few feet away from a statue of Mary. The stone read: "Praying for Peace and Unity. Remembering the Orlando Victims: 12 June 2016. *Recordemos, creamos.*"

So increasing numbers of parishes are welcoming too.

Still, what is the Christian response if some LGBT Catholics feel continuing hostility toward select Catholic leaders?

By way of a suggestion, let me tell you a story. When I was twenty-seven, I told my parents I was entering the Jesuits. I sprang the news on them with absolutely no warning; I hadn't even told them I was considering it. Not surprisingly, they were confused and upset. They saw the decision as reckless. And that confused and upset me.

I wondered, *How can they not see what I am doing? How*

*can they not understand me?* In response, my spiritual director said, "You've had twenty-seven years to get used to this, Jim. And you just sprung it on them. Give them the gift of time."

Challenging as it may be to hear, and without setting aside the immense suffering LGBT people have experienced in the church, I wonder if the LGBT community could continue to give the institutional church the gift of time—time to get to know each other. In a real way, an open and public LGBT community is a new thing, even in my lifetime. In a real way, the world is just getting to know that community. So is the church.

It's a decided burden, but it's perhaps not surprising. It takes time to get to know people. So perhaps the LGBT community can continue to give the institutional church the gift of patience.

If, even after all this, some people still perceive a few church leaders as enemies, the deeper Christian response is to pray for them. And that's not me speaking, that's the Jesus of the Gospels, who said, "Love your enemies and pray for those who persecute you" (Matt. 5:44–48; Lk. 6:27–36).

What do I mean by praying for them? Not simply the condescending prayer that says "God, help them not to be such terrible people" but a sincere prayer for their well-being. Of course, we can pray for a person's conversion, for *metanoia*, particularly someone who seems unwilling to show mercy and compassion toward others, but prayer should always be done with a loving heart. True prayer wants others to flourish.

If any Catholics still have a hard time praying for church leaders, they might use a prayer that I find helpful when I am struggling with another person. My prayer is to see that person as God sees him or her.

This prayer, in my experience, is always answered.

# Sensitivity

L et's return to the beautiful word *sensitivity*. Again, we can use it to mean not denigrating the bishops or the hierarchy. And again, that is not only simple human courtesy; it is Christian charity. But I would like to use *sensitivity* in another way. I would like to invite the LGBT community to more deeply consider who is speaking and how they are speaking. Here I'm turning to theology—specifically ecclesiology, the branch of Christian theology that looks at the church itself. I would like to focus on the theological idea—which is a traditional part of Catholic teaching—of the different "levels of authority."

As Catholics, we believe in various levels of teaching authority in our church. Not every church official speaks with the same level of authority. The simplest way of explaining this is that what your local pastor says in a homily does not come from the same level of authority as what the pope says in an encyclical. The different levels of authoritative teaching begin with the Gospels, which are followed by the documents of church councils and then papal pronouncements. Even the different papal pronouncements have various levels of authority. Among those with the highest authority are constitutions or encyclicals, addressed to the whole church; followed by apostolic letters and *motu proprios*; then the pope's daily homilies, speeches, and press conferences; and so on. There are also documents from synods and individual Vatican congregations and, on the local level, documents from bishops' conferences and pastoral letters from local bishops. Each has a different level of authority. They all need to be prayerfully read and studied, but it is important to know that they do not all have equal authority.

Of course, the hierarchy is not the only group that speaks with authority. Authority resides in holiness as well. Holy men and women who are not members of the hierarchy, like Saint Teresa of Calcutta, and holy laypeople, like Dorothy Day or Jean Vanier, speak with authority.

Also, it's important to be careful about taking what the mainstream media says about "church teachings" at face value. Recently I read a headline that said, "Keep

Homilies to Eight Minutes, Vatican Tells Clergy." I thought, *The Vatican says this?* Sure enough, when I read the article, I discovered that the supposed instructions came from an individual bishop working in the Vatican who was offering his own suggestions to preachers. The headline was false. The "Vatican" wasn't doing any such thing. So again, sensitivity is in order.

Moreover, we need to be sensitive to the fact that when Vatican officials speak—whether it is the pope or a Vatican congregation—they are speaking to the entire world, not just the West and certainly not just the United States. A statement that seems tepid in the United States might be shocking in parts of Latin America or Sub-Saharan Africa.

To that end, I was disappointed in the reaction of some LGBT Catholics in the United States to the pope's apostolic exhortation on family life, *Amoris Laetitia,* "The Joy of Love."

In that document, Pope Francis says:

We would like before all else to reaffirm that every person, regardless of sexual orientation, ought to be respected in his or her dignity and treated with consideration, while "every sign of unjust discrimination" is to be carefully avoided, particularly any form of aggression and violence. Such families should be given respectful pastoral guidance, so that those who manifest a homosexual orientation can receive the assistance they need to understand and fully carry out God's will in their lives (No. 250).

*"Before all else,"* the pope says, LGBT people should be treated with dignity. That's an immense statement, and by the way, nowhere does he mention anything about an "objective disorder." Nonetheless, among some LGBT people in this country those lines were dismissed with cries of "Not enough!"

Perhaps in the West those words seemed insufficient. But the pope is writing not simply for the West, much less simply for the United States. Imagine reading that in a country where violence against LGBT people is rampant or even the norm, or where LGBT people have been jailed or executed, and the Catholic Church has remained silent. What seems tepid in the United States is incendiary in other parts of the world. What seems obvious to a bishop in one country is a clear, forceful, or even threatening challenge to a bishop in another country. What seems arid to LGBT people in one country may be, to those in another country, water in a barren desert.

By the same token, there is a role for prophecy. Prophets are sometimes called to say things that make others uncomfortable, even angry, out of their love for God and others. The prophet both points people ahead to the future that God promises and calls them back to the source of their love: God. Yet prophetic speech does not have to devolve into yelling and shaming.

Doubtless many readers will think of Jesus turning over the tables of the money changers in the Temple or excoriating religious leaders of his day: "But woe to you, scribes and Pharisees, hypocrites! For you lock people out of the kingdom of heaven" (Matt. 23:13). Or John the Baptist, standing in his camel-hair garment by the Jordan River, doing the same: "[W]hen he saw many Pharisees and Sadducees coming for baptism, he said to them, 'You brood of vipers! Who warned you to flee from the wrath to come?'" (Matt. 3:7).

There is a place for this kind of prophecy, and it has been exercised by some of the greatest saints in the Christian tradition. But it must be exercised with great care. For none of us is John the Baptist, the ascetical prophet, much less Jesus, the sinless one.

I'm certainly not saying that one should never be angry. Anger is a natural and healthy human emotion, as well as a legitimate and even necessary response to injustice. Jesus himself was angered when he saw injustice, especially when it was committed against people on the margins. And some of the greatest prophets of our time have been moved by a righteous anger.

Moreover, many LGBT Catholics have a right to be angry. Can anyone blame them for their anger after having been insulted, marginalized, and excluded over the years? These experiences lead many to desire justice for themselves and other LGBT Catholics, and this desire is expressed in different ways.

As Jason Steidl, an openly gay Catholic theologian, pointed out to me, there are different kinds of prophetic works that need to be done, depending on the individual or group and their "charism," the Christian term for a specific gift (from the Greek *charisma*). Here he was recalling St. Paul's image of the church as a body, with each member possessing different gifts and callings.

"Each group or person does something different," Jason wrote to me, "and each group or person has a charism that reflects their relationship to the hierarchy and their access to institutional power."

That was an important insight for me to hear because as a priest I have connections to members of the hierarchy that others may not have. Although I believe that quiet dialogue is the most fruitful means of building a bridge, calls for this can ring hollow to LGBT people who feel blocked from any avenues of engagement with the hierarchy. In other words, they feel that the lanes to the bridge are simply closed to them. They would welcome speaking with their local bishop but for many reasons are unable to do so, and this inability increases their frustration and sense of exclusion. Thus, the only outlets they feel are available are activities like public protests.

Jason wrote this reflection, expanding on the image of the church as a body:

> A cry of pain from a stubbed toe is far healthier than feeling no pain at all. In the first instance, the body works as it ought to bring healing. The toe is still fully a part of the body and is alive. In the second case, the toe is dead or perhaps gangrenous or leprous. The whole body could die from blood poisoning. The stakes are high, but I trust that God has us all where we are to use the gifts that God has given us to work for change.

But all those who feel called to prophetic ministry, and even protest, are invited to do it from a place of deep and authentic love. They are called to ask themselves: *Is this true prophecy? Where does the desire to be prophetic come from? How is God in this? Am I doing this out of love?*

Prophets are always motivated by love, and not only of individuals, but often of the institution. The Franciscan spiritual writer Richard Rohr, OFM, writes this about true prophecy:

> Prophets, by their very nature, cannot be at the center of any social structure. Rather, they are "on the edge of the inside." They cannot be fully insiders, but they cannot throw rocks from outside either. They must be educated inside the system, knowing and living the rules, before they can critique what is nonessential or not so important. Jesus did this masterfully (see Matt. 5:17–48). This is what Martin Luther King, Jr., taught the United States, what Gandhi taught British-occupied India, and what Nelson Mandela taught South Africa. . . . A prophet critiques a system by quoting its own documents, constitutions, heroes, and Scriptures against its present practice. This is their secret: systems are best unlocked from inside.

All of us need to discern carefully, even during those times when we feel called to be prophetic. So we are called to be sensitive in many ways.

# Together on the Bridge

You've been invited to walk on a bridge built on the three pillars of the *Catechism*'s approach to LGBT ministry: respect, compassion, and sensitivity.

Some of this may be hard for members of the LGBT community to hear. Some of this also may be hard for bishops and Catholic leaders to hear. This is because neither lane on that bridge is smooth. On this bridge, as in life, there are tolls. It costs when you live a life of respect, compassion, and sensitivity. But to trust in that bridge is to trust that eventually people will be able to cross back and forth easily, and that the hierarchy and the LGBT community will be able to encounter one another, accompany one another, and love one another.

To trust in that bridge is also to trust that God desires forgiveness. It is to trust that God desires reconciliation. It is to trust that God desires unity.

We are all on the bridge together, for that bridge is the

church. And, ultimately, on the other side of the bridge for each group is welcome, community, and love.

In conclusion, I would like to say something specifically to LGBT Catholics. In difficult times you might ask: "What keeps the bridge standing? What keeps it from collapsing onto the sharp rocks? What keeps us from plunging into the treacherous waters below?"

The answer is the Holy Spirit.

The Holy Spirit, which is supporting the church, is supporting *you,* for you are beloved children of God who, by virtue of your baptism, have as much right to be in the church as the pope, your local bishop, and me.

The bridge that I am inviting you to traverse has some loose stones, big bumps, and deep potholes, because the people in our church are not perfect. We never have been— just ask Saint Peter. And we never will be. We are all imperfect people, struggling to do our best in the light of our individual vocations. We are all pilgrims on the way, loved sinners following the call we heard first at our baptism and that we continue to hear every day.

In short, you are not alone. Millions of your Catholic brothers and sisters accompany you, as do many of the leaders of your church, as we journey imperfectly together on this bridge.

More important, you are accompanied by God, the reconciler of all men and women, as well as the architect, the builder, and the foundation of that bridge.

# Biblical Passages
# for Reflection
# and Meditation

Whh discussing controversial topics with those with whom we disagree it is sometimes easy to lose track of what we hold in common. All Christians have access to the spiritual riches found in the Scriptures, which, after all, were written amid the spiritual turmoil and social conflicts of the writers' times. We can learn from those who went before us. That is one reason why active reflection and meditation on Scripture can be such a rich and illuminating spiritual practice.

In this section of the book I have collected biblical passages, as spiritual resources for members of the LGBT community, with accompanying questions that can serve as aids to personal or communal reflection. The first group includes passages referred to in the essay "A Two-Way Bridge." Later come passages that I have found, through my ministry, consistently speak to LGBT people and their families and friends. All these beautiful passages are not just for LGBT people but can be used by everyone, especially those who hope to welcome them more fully into community.

You can use these passages in any way you wish, but let me offer a few suggestions.

*First,* after each passage or group of passages on the same topic, I have provided reflection questions to help you meditate more deeply about what these passages might say to you. Remember that God speaks powerfully through the Bible, the living word of God. You might think about these questions and then imagine yourself in God's presence (which you always are, but you are more conscious of it when you pray) and share your answers with God. Some find "journaling"—writing down what happens in your prayer—helpful. Some even find writing a letter to God helpful.

*Second,* one of the spiritual traditions of my religious order is a technique popularized by Saint Ignatius Loyola, the founder of the Jesuits, in which you imagine yourself in a Scripture scene with as much vividness as possible. You ask yourself: "What do I see? What do I hear? What do I feel? What do I smell? What do I taste?" With God's help, you try to "place" yourself in the Bible scene imaginatively.

This method of prayer may strike you as odd, but since your imagination is one of God's gifts to you, God can work through it. Often this technique can help you see the passage in a more personal way. You might, for example, be reading about Jesus healing a sick person, recognize the need for healing in your own life, and be moved to ask God for help in that area.

For some passages, this technique may not work as well—Saint Paul's letters, for example, are in general not stories but didactic missives. They may lend themselves more to a kind of quiet meditation, where the primary fruit of prayer is a new insight or a deeper understanding. But in the Old and New Testaments, many passages lend themselves easily to the imaginative kind of "Ignatian" prayer. In the stories of Jesus encountering people with a variety of hopes and desires, try to imagine yourself in the scene and see what sort of feelings, memories, insights, desires, and emotions arise in you. Then pay attention to them and share what happens in prayer with God.

*Third,* you might allow God to speak to you in a quieter way. That is, you might simply sit silently with a passage, or even a single word, without needing to imagine yourself in any "scene." The prayer here is less concerned with images and is more free-form. Then you might discover that the passage evokes a feeling of calm or comfort, or a desire to act or advocate. See in those feelings and desires God's reaching out to you.

In the end, there is no "right" way to pray. The right

way is what works best for you. And whatever way you use these passages is up to you.

*Finally,* the reflection questions can be used in group settings as either discussion topics or aids to communal prayer. I've included questions for LGBT people as well as their families, friends, and allies.

That last set of questions—for families, friends, and allies—is designed for a group that is sometimes overlooked in the church. Remember the elderly woman who told me that she simply wanted a place in the church for her transgender grandchild? She reminded me that ministry to LGBT people is a ministry not simply to the relatively small percentage of Catholics who are LGBT but to their parents and grandparents, brothers and sisters, aunts and uncles, as well as their friends and neighbors, coworkers and roommates.

So these Bible passages, meditations, and reflection questions are also for them, as they consider the ways in which they too relate to God.

# On Names and Naming

Names are important in the Old and New Testaments. Names often communicate something essential about a person. "Isaac," for example, the name of the son of Abraham and Sarah, means "He laughs" or "laughter," since Sarah had laughed when she heard the improbable news that she would bear a son in her old age (Gen. 18:12). The name "Jesus" (Yeshua) means "The Lord saves." To know another person's name was to have a certain level of knowledge of, intimacy with, and even power over the person. Let's consider some of the more significant biblical passages on names and naming.

*God allows Adam ("the man") to name the creatures:*

> So out of the ground the LORD God formed every animal of the field and every bird of the air, and

brought them to the man to see what he would call them; and whatever the man called each living creature, that was its name. The man gave names to all cattle, and to the birds of the air, and to every animal of the field (Gen. 2:19–20).

*God renames Abram:*

No longer shall your name be Abram, but your name shall be Abraham; for I have made you the ancestor of a multitude of nations (Gen. 17:5).

*Moses asks to know God's name:*

Then the LORD said [to Moses], "I have observed the misery of my people who are in Egypt; I have heard their cry on account of their taskmasters. So come, I will send you to Pharaoh to bring my people, the Israelites, out of Egypt." But Moses said to God, "If I come to the Israelites and say to them, 'The God of your ancestors has sent me to you,' and they ask me, 'What is his name?' what shall I say to them?" God said to Moses, "I AM WHO I AM." He said further, "Thus you shall say to the Israelites, 'I AM has sent me to you.'" God also said to

Moses, "Thus you shall say to the Israelites, 'The LORD, the God of your ancestors, the God of Abraham, the God of Isaac, and the God of Jacob, has sent me to you'" (Exod. 3:7, 10, 13–15).

## Reflection Questions

1. By what name do you call God? *Lord? Creator? Friend?* What is God's name for you?

2. Can you name a few of the people who have been the most helpful in your spiritual journey? Name them in God's presence and offer thanks for their help.

3. When you think of your own sexual orientation or gender identity, what word do you use? Why? Can you speak to God about this in prayer?

4. What was it like for you to "come out" or share your sexuality or identity for the first time? What was that "naming" like for you? Can you share with God your experiences, both positive and negative? Can you rejoice with God over the positive ones, and grieve with God over the negative ones?

5. Try imagining yourself, in prayer, in Moses's place. What would it be like to talk to God directly? How do you think you might feel while God spoke? What would you have said or asked?

6. *For families, friends, and allies:* How did you feel when you first heard your family member or friend "name" his or her sexuality or gender identity? Did that "naming" change or deepen your relationship with that person? What does that say to you about your own relationship with God?

# Different Gifts

In the First Letter to the Corinthians, Saint Paul presents an image of the church as a body whose members all contribute to its functioning. All of us bring different gifts to the church, no matter who we are. Some of us have a gift for organization and we arrange events. Others have a talent for music and serve in liturgical settings. Others of us love theology and use it to explain our faith to others. All of us make up the Body of Christ, a traditional image of the church.

Notice how Saint Paul focuses on the parts of the body that are seen as "less honorable." Sometimes LGBT people are, tragically, made to feel that way in the church and in society, but, as Paul says, it is precisely these people who deserve even greater respect.

For just as the body is one and has many members, and all the members of the body, though many, are one body, so it is with Christ. For in the one Spirit we were all baptized into one body—Jews or Greeks, slaves or free—and we were all made to drink of one Spirit.

Indeed, the body does not consist of one member but of many. If the foot were to say, "Because I am not a hand, I do not belong to the body," that would not make it any less a part of the body. And if the ear were to say, "Because I am not an eye, I do not belong to the body," that would not make it any less a part of the body. If the whole body were an eye, where would the hearing be? If the whole body were hearing, where would the sense of smell be? But as it is, God arranged the members in the body, each one of them, as he chose. If all were a single member, where would the body be? As it is, there are many members, yet one body. The eye cannot say to the hand, "I have no need of you," nor again the head to the feet, "I have no need of you." On the contrary, the members of the body that seem to be weaker are indispensable, and those members of the body that we think less honorable we clothe with greater honor, and our less respectable members are treated with greater respect; whereas our more respectable members do not need this. But God has so arranged the body, giving the greater honor to the inferior member, that there may be no dissension within the body, but the members may have the same care for one another. If one member suffers, all suffer together with it; if one member is honored, all rejoice together with it.

Now you are the body of Christ and individually members of it (1 Cor. 12:12–27).

## Reflection Questions

1. Saint Paul speaks powerfully of the different gifts that every member of the church brings and can contribute to the church. What gifts do you bring? Can you thank God for these gifts?

2. How have you exercised these gifts?

3. Has anyone ever prevented you from exercising your gifts in the church? Can you express how you feel about that to God?

4. Paul says that the "members" of the body (or church) who have been the least respected should be honored the most. Does that make sense to you?

5. Do you feel like you are a part of the "body" of the church? Why or why not? What, or who, helps you to feel more a part of the church? When have you most felt a part of the church?

6. What gifts from others in the church have helped you move closer to God? That is, who has helped you on your journey?

7. *For families, friends, and allies:* How have LGBT people brought their gifts to your life and your ministry? How do you recognize those gifts? Has your ministry lost out on gifts because of prejudices? What might you do to combat those prejudices?

# Care for Those Who Are Persecuted

Most people know Jesus's Parable of the Good Samaritan, but after spending time reflecting on it, many can still be surprised by it. After all, a parable is not meant to have only one meaning. The biblical scholar C. H. Dodd wrote, in a well-known definition, that a parable "teases the mind into active thought." Parables, one of the primary ways that Jesus taught, are stories designed to open one's mind and heart to the mystery of God.

For me, this famous parable shows us not only the need to care for those who are persecuted but also how help can come from someone completely unexpected. The Samaritans were, for a number of reasons, considered enemies by many of the Jewish people. So there is a turnaround here: in this story Jesus names the outsider as the hero.

Moreover, the person we hate turns out to be the person we need.

> Just then a lawyer stood up to test Jesus. "Teacher," he said, "what must I do to inherit eternal life?" He said to him, "What is written in the law? What do you read there?" He answered, "You shall love the LORD your God with all your heart, and with all your soul, and with all your strength, and with all your mind; and your neighbor as yourself." And he said to him, "You have given the right answer; do this, and you will live."
>
> But wanting to justify himself, he asked Jesus, "And who is my neighbor?" Jesus replied, "A man was going down from Jerusalem to Jericho, and fell into the hands of robbers, who stripped him, beat him, and went away, leaving him half dead. Now by chance a priest was going down that road; and when he saw him, he passed by on the other side. So likewise a Levite, when he came to the place and saw him, passed by on the other side. But a Samaritan while traveling came near him; and when he saw him,

he was moved with pity. He went to him and bandaged his wounds, having poured oil and wine on them. Then he put him on his own animal, brought him to an inn, and took care of him. The next day he took out two denarii, gave them to the innkeeper, and said, 'Take care of him; and when I come back, I will repay you whatever more you spend.' Which of these three, do you think, was a neighbor to the man who fell into the hands of the robbers?" He said, "The one who showed him mercy." Jesus said to him, "Go and do likewise" (Lk. 10:25–37).

## Reflection Questions

1. When have you been a Good Samaritan to someone else?

2. When has someone unexpected or surprising cared for you?

3. The great turnaround in this story is that the person who would seem to be the least likely to help not only helps but goes the extra mile. Has anyone you hated ever unexpectedly helped you?

4. Has anyone ever "passed by" when you needed help? Why do you think their hearts were closed? Can you pray to understand them, even to forgive them?

5. Think of individuals you dislike, perhaps in the church. Can you pray that one day you might be a Good Samaritan to them? And can you pray that one day you might be open to receiving help from them in some way?

6. In what ways has God "bandaged" your wounds?

7. *For families, friends, and allies:* How have LGBT people been Good Samaritans to you? How are you called to be a Good Samaritan in return? Have you ever experienced any surprises in your relationships with your LGBT friends or family members? What does that say to you about God?

# Jesus Meets People
# Where They Are

In the story of Jesus's healing of the Roman centurion's servant, notice that Jesus does not castigate the Roman centurion for not being Jewish. Nor does he shout "Pagan!" Rather, Jesus accepts the centurion as he is and does what the man requests: he heals his servant. He also lavishly praises the faith of a person who would have been seen, at the time, as the ultimate outsider. Finally, Jesus is open to being *surprised* by someone on the margins.

> When [Jesus] entered Capernaum, a centurion
> came to him, appealing to him and saying,
> "Lord, my servant is lying at home paralyzed,
> in terrible distress." And he said to him, "I will

come and cure him." The centurion answered, "Lord, I am not worthy to have you come under my roof; but only speak the word, and my servant will be healed. For I also am a man under authority, with soldiers under me; and I say to one, 'Go,' and he goes, and to another, 'Come,' and he comes, and to my slave, 'Do this,' and the slave does it." When Jesus heard him, he was amazed and said to those who followed him, "Truly I tell you, in no one in Israel have I found such faith. I tell you, many will come from east and west and will eat with Abraham and Isaac and Jacob in the kingdom of heaven, while the heirs of the kingdom will be thrown into the outer darkness, where there will be weeping and gnashing of teeth." And to the centurion Jesus said, "Go; let it be done for you according to your faith." And the servant was healed in that hour (Matt. 8:5–13).

## Reflection Questions

1. Does it surprise you that Jesus helped someone who was a "pagan"? What do you think the reac-

tion of those around him might have been? What enables Jesus to encounter the man so freely?

2. What do you think enabled the Roman centurion to approach Jesus?

3. What does Jesus's welcome of the centurion say to you about God's welcome?

4. When you imagine this story, what do you think the centurion's response was to this encounter with Jesus? Have you ever experienced a surprising welcome? What kind of healing has God offered you?

5. Jesus praises the centurion's faith as greater than that of everyone in Israel. What does the centurion's faith say to you? How can it influence your own?

6. *For families, friends, and allies:* Your family member or friend has confided in you and relied on you. Have you ever been "amazed," as Jesus was, by the trust that has been placed in you? How does that make you feel toward the one who trusts you? Toward God? Notice that the centurion is asking for help for someone else. How does this intersect with your own relationship with your LGBT family member or friend?

Likewise, as you'll see in the following passage, when Jesus meets Zacchaeus, the chief tax collector in Jericho, Jesus does not castigate the person who would have been considered the "chief sinner" in the area. Rather, he encounters him and offers to visit his home, a public sign of welcome that leads to the man's change of heart. For Jesus, it is most often community first, conversion second.

Also notice that Zacchaeus, like so many of us, simply wants to see "who Jesus was." How touching a detail that is! And how like so many LGBT people today, who simply want to encounter Jesus. But the "crowd" prevents him from doing so, just as the crowd often does with LGBT people today. Undeterred, Zacchaeus goes to great lengths to see Jesus, by literally going out on a limb.

After Jesus's dramatic words of welcome, the people of the town show their disapproval by beginning to "grumble." But Zacchaeus "stood there." The original Greek word *statheis,* however, may be closer to "stood his ground." The extension of mercy to a person on the margins usually causes grumbling from those on the "inside." As it does today! It's a reminder not to let those who grumble stand in the way of an encounter with Jesus. Remember Pope Francis's comment: "For Jesus what matters above all is reaching out to save those far off, healing the wounds of the sick, restoring everyone to God's family! And this is scandalous to some people!"

This transformative experience, this direct encounter with mercy and compassion, leads to Zacchaeus's conversion—the kind of conversion of minds and hearts to which all of us are called.

> [Jesus] entered Jericho and was passing through it. A man was there named Zacchaeus; he was a chief tax collector and was rich. He was trying to see who Jesus was, but on account of the crowd he could not, because he was short in stature. So he ran ahead and climbed a sycamore tree to see him, because he was going to pass that way. When Jesus came to the place, he looked up and said to him, "Zacchaeus, hurry and come down; for I must stay at your house today." So he hurried down and was happy to welcome him. All who saw it began to grumble and said, "He has gone to be the guest of one who is a sinner." Zacchaeus stood there and said to the Lord, "Look, half of my possessions, Lord,

I will give to the poor; and if I have defrauded anyone of anything, I will pay back four times as much." Then Jesus said to him, "Today salvation has come to this house, because he too is a son of Abraham. For the Son of Man came to seek out and to save the lost" (Lk. 19:1–10).

## Reflection Questions

1. Zacchaeus climbed out on a limb because he wanted to see "who Jesus was." Who is Jesus for you? How have you been able to "see" him in your life?

2. The tax collector could not see "on account of the crowd." This probably refers to Zacchaeus being "short in stature" but it can also be a powerful image of people whose opinions or opposition stand in our way. When have others, or the opinions of others, prevented you from moving closer to God?

3. The insight about "community first, conversion second" comes from the biblical scholar Ben Meyer. He contrasts Jesus's approach to that of John the

Baptist, who asked for repentance first. Of course, we all need to repent and are all called to continual conversion, but what does Jesus's approach say to you about the church? And about you?

4. Zacchaeus is moved to conversion in this story. This is the *metanoia*, or conversion of minds and hearts, that we are all called to. What kinds of changes in your life is God inviting you to?

5. *For families, friends, and allies:* The crowd begins to "grumble" when Jesus offers Zacchaeus welcome. That is, they oppose Jesus's outreach. When have you stood up for your LGBT family member or friend in the face of grumbling? Have you ever thought of your support as the work of Jesus? Perhaps you might share this experience with Jesus in prayer.

# You Are
# "Wonderfully Made"

In Psalm 139, the psalmist tells us that God created us, knows us intimately, and understands us. The image of God knitting us together in our mothers' wombs is a vivid reminder that we are "wonderfully made" by the God who created us. Of all the passages in the Bible, this one, in my experience, has proven to be the most helpful for LGBT people and their family and friends.

O LORD, you have searched me and known me.
You know when I sit down and when I rise up;
    you discern my thoughts from far away.
You search out my path and my lying down,
    and are acquainted with all my ways.

Even before a word is on my tongue,
    O LORD, you know it completely.
You hem me in, behind and before,
    and lay your hand upon me.
Such knowledge is too wonderful for me;
    it is so high that I cannot attain it.

Where can I go from your spirit?
    Or where can I flee from your presence?
If I ascend to heaven, you are there;
    if I make my bed in Sheol, you are
        there.
If I take the wings of the morning
    and settle at the farthest limits of the sea,
even there your hand shall lead me,
    and your right hand shall hold me fast.
If I say, "Surely the darkness shall cover me,
    and the light around me become night,"
even the darkness is not dark to you;
    the night is as bright as the day,
    for darkness is as light to you.

For it was you who formed my inward parts;
    you knit me together in my mother's
        womb.

I praise you, for I am fearfully and wonderfully
made.
Wonderful are your works;
that I know very well.
My frame was not hidden from you,
when I was being made in secret,
intricately woven in the depths of the
earth.
Your eyes beheld my unformed substance.
In your book were written
all the days that were formed for me,
when none of them as yet existed.
How weighty to me are your thoughts, O God!
How vast is the sum of them!
I try to count them—they are more than the
sand;
I come to the end—I am still with you.

(PSALM 139:1–18)

## Reflection Questions

1. Think about what it means for you to be "wonderfully made." Can you praise God, as the psalmist does? What would your praise look like?

2. What is it like to think of God forming you in your "mother's womb"?

3. The psalmist admits that God's ways are beyond the human capacity to understand, and yet the psalmist is "still with" God. What do you think gives the psalmist that kind of faith?

4. God, who creates only good things, made your "inward parts." How does that make you feel about yourself? Can you tell God in your own words how you feel?

5. Saint Augustine said, "God is nearer to me than I am to myself" (*interior intimo meo*). What is it like to imagine God knowing you so intimately, as the psalmist does?

6. The psalmist writes: "[E]ven the darkness is not dark to you; / the night is as bright as the day, / for darkness is as light to you." What do those lines say to you?

7. *For families, friends, and allies:* You are "wonderfully made" yourself! And your family member or friend is made in a different, but no less wonderful, way. What does this say to you about God's "works" and God's "thoughts"?

# God Is Your Strength

In times of persecution, rejection, and struggle, Psalm 62 has often helped my LGBT friends find some solace, rest, and strength. It can also be a balm to family members and allies who may themselves feel the need for consolation.

> For God alone my soul waits in silence;
> from him comes my salvation.
> He alone is my rock and my salvation,
> my fortress; I shall never be shaken.
> How long will you assail a person,
> will you batter your victim, all of you,
> as you would a leaning wall, a tottering fence?
> Their only plan is to bring down a person of
> prominence.
> They take pleasure in falsehood;

they bless with their mouths,
  but inwardly they curse.

For God alone my soul waits in silence,
  for my hope is from him.
He alone is my rock and my salvation,
  my fortress; I shall not be shaken.
On God rests my deliverance and my honor;
  my mighty rock, my refuge is in God.
Trust in him at all times, O people;
  pour out your heart before him;
  God is a refuge for us.

Those of low estate are but a breath,
  those of high estate are a delusion;
in the balances they go up;
  they are together lighter than a breath.
Put no confidence in extortion,
  and set no vain hopes on robbery;
  if riches increase, do not set your heart on
    them.

Once God has spoken;
  twice have I heard this:
that power belongs to God,
  and steadfast love belongs to you, O Lord.

**For you repay to all**
**according to their work.**

## Reflection Questions

1.  What image appeals most to you in this psalm: God as *salvation*, *rock*, *fortress*, or *refuge*? Why?

2.  As you look back over your life, in what ways has God been your "strength"?

3.  "They take pleasure in falsehood; / they bless with their mouths, / but inwardly they curse." These harsh words from the psalmist are directed toward individuals and groups who have shown him no love or compassion. He is speaking honestly to God about people who have harmed him or his people. Can you trust God enough to complain, as the psalmist does, about the people who have "cursed" you? Can you trust that God will hear all your prayers?

4.  What does it mean to "pour out" your heart to God? Can you do that now in prayer, confident that God hears you?

5. *For families, friends, and allies:* The process of accepting the sexuality of a family member or friend
can be challenging. In what ways has God been
your "rock"? How can God be a "rock" for you in
the future?

# Jesus Proclaims
# His Identity

When Jesus enters the synagogue in Nazareth to preach from the Hebrew Scriptures and announce his identity and mission, he probably knows how his fellow townspeople will respond. After all, for thirty years he lived among them in the small town of Nazareth (with a population of only two to four hundred people in Jesus's time). Despite that, he boldly proclaims who he is and what he stands for.

Many LGBT people have told me that this passage has helped them accept and "own" their identity in the face of misunderstanding and opposition, even from those who are closest to them. And make no mistake: the townspeople are furious at Jesus, going so far as to attempt to "hurl him off the cliff." Knowing of their

probable reaction, Jesus says what he needs to say anyway. The passage is often called the "Rejection at Nazareth," but I like to think of it as the "Proclamation of
Jesus's Identity."

> When he came to Nazareth, where he had been
> brought up, he went to the synagogue on the
> sabbath day, as was his custom. He stood up to
> read, and the scroll of the prophet Isaiah was
> given to him. He unrolled the scroll and found
> the place where it was written:

> "The Spirit of the LORD is upon me,
>        because he has anointed me
>             to bring good news to the poor.
> He has sent me to proclaim release to the
>    captives
>        and recovery of sight to the blind,
>             to let the oppressed go free,
> to proclaim the year of the LORD's favor."

> And he rolled up the scroll, gave it back to
> the attendant, and sat down. The eyes of all
> in the synagogue were fixed on him. Then he

began to say to them, "Today this scripture has been fulfilled in your hearing." All spoke well of him and were amazed at the gracious words that came from his mouth. They said, "Is not this Joseph's son?" He said to them, "Doubtless you will quote to me this proverb, 'Doctor, cure yourself!' And you will say, 'Do here also in your hometown the things that we have heard you did at Capernaum.'" And he said, "Truly I tell you, no prophet is accepted in the prophet's hometown. But the truth is, there were many widows in Israel in the time of Elijah, when the heaven was shut up for three years and six months, and there was a severe famine over all the land; yet Elijah was sent to none of them except to a widow at Zarephath in Sidon. There were also many lepers in Israel in the time of the prophet Elisha, and none of them was cleansed except Naaman the Syrian." When they heard this, all in the synagogue were filled with rage. They got up, drove him out of the town, and led him to the brow of the hill on which their town was built, so that they might hurl him off the cliff. But he passed through the midst of them and went on his way (Lk. 4:16–30).

## Reflection Questions

1. Do you think it was difficult for Jesus to proclaim his identity in front of people who knew him so well?

2. What do you think enabled Jesus to do this? What enables you to accept yourself as you are? Have you spoken about your sexuality or identity with anyone yet? If not, what might Jesus's example say to you?

3. Jesus faced fierce opposition both here in his hometown and later in his ministry elsewhere. Opposition from the people closest to us can be painful. Have you ever been rejected outright? Can you speak to Jesus about that pain? Can you let him speak to you?

4. After this rejection at Nazareth, Jesus finds people who are eager to hear his word in the towns and villages around the Sea of Galilee. What have been your places of rejection? What have been your places of acceptance?

5. Jesus knows what it is like to be rejected. How does this make you feel toward him? Can you share that with him in prayer?

6. *For families, friends, and allies:* What was it like for you when your family member or friend first shared his or her sexuality with you? Have you ever known people who wanted to, figuratively, hurl that person off a cliff? What was your reaction?

# Jesus Calls Peter

Sometimes we doubt that we are "worthy" of following Jesus or being loved by God. But all of us—straight, gay, lesbian, bisexual, transgender—are imperfect. All of us have our flaws. All of us sin. Yet God calls all of us. Peter's response is typical—aware of our sinfulness, we feel unworthy in the face of God's call and unworthy of God's generosity. But Jesus calls us anyway.

> Once while Jesus was standing beside the lake of Gennesaret, and the crowd was pressing in on him to hear the word of God, he saw two boats there at the shore of the lake; the fishermen had gone out of them and were washing their nets. He got into one of the

boats, the one belonging to Simon, and asked him to put out a little way from the shore. Then he sat down and taught the crowds from the boat. When he had finished speaking, he said to Simon, "Put out into the deep water and let down your nets for a catch." Simon answered, "Master, we have worked all night long but have caught nothing. Yet if you say so, I will let down the nets." When they had done this, they caught so many fish that their nets were beginning to break. So they signaled their partners in the other boat to come and help them. And they came and filled both boats, so that they began to sink. But when Simon Peter saw it, he fell down at Jesus's knees, saying, "Go away from me, Lord, for I am a sinful man!" For he and all who were with him were amazed at the catch of fish that they had taken; and so also were James and John, sons of Zebedee, who were partners with Simon. Then Jesus said to Simon, "Do not be afraid; from now on you will be catching people." When they had brought their boats to shore, they left everything and followed him (Lk. 5:1–11).

## Reflection Questions

1. In the face of the divine, Peter (here called Simon, his original name) naturally feels his imperfections. Bill Creed, a Jesuit spiritual director, once described this common experience by saying, "In the sunshine of God's love, we see our shadows." What are the "shadows" in your life? Can you bring them before God in prayer, as Peter does here?

2. Nets bursting with fish is a powerful image of the abundance of blessings that God has given us—and will give us. This abundance helps to enable Peter to trust in Jesus. If you were to list your blessings, what would be in your "net"?

3. Peter says he had worked all night and caught nothing. Without Jesus, we can do nothing. With him, we can do everything. Where could you use Jesus's help? Can you ask for it in prayer?

4. Jesus knows that Peter is imperfect, and yet he calls him anyway. We are all imperfect—struggling people trying to do our best. As Jesuits like to say, we are all "loved sinners." Do you believe God can call you even with your imperfections?

5. *For families, friends, and allies:* You have many "calls" in your life. One is to love your family members and friends in all their complexity. But sometimes you might feel inadequate to the task, as Peter did. What helps you love and support your LGBT family members and friends? What "catch of fish" encourages you?

# Jesus and the
# Samaritan Woman

Time and again in the Gospels, Jesus reaches out to people who find themselves on the margins of society and he offers them welcome—in this case, a Samaritan woman. Tensions between Jews and Samaritans (that is, people of the region of Samaria, between Judea and Galilee) had existed for centuries, primarily based on religious differences. "Jews do not share things in common with Samaritans," says the Gospel here, underlining the point. So, as Francis J. Moloney, SDB, a New Testament scholar, says in his commentary on the Gospel of John, "On two accounts Jesus should not speak to her: she is a woman and she is a Samaritan."

In addition, the "woman at the well" has been married several times, and is apparently living with someone who is not her husband, so she may bear a social stigma as a result. Some commentators have suggested that the reason she visits the well at "about noon," in the heat of the day, is because of embarrassment: this is when other women would not be present. She also professes some suspicion of (or surprise over) Jesus, asking him why he is talking with her.

None of this seems to bother Jesus. Notice how he encounters someone who has felt marginalized, how he reveals his full identity to her, and how she responds. In response to his welcome, she opens up to him, sharing not only her story but also her desire for the "living water" that he brings—and that he is.

After he listens to her and shares something meaningful about himself, she becomes an "apostle," someone sent to bring the Good News to others.

> [Jesus] left Judea and started back to Galilee. But he had to go through Samaria. So he came to a Samaritan city called Sychar, near the plot of ground that Jacob had given to his son Joseph. Jacob's well was there, and Jesus, tired out by his journey, was sitting by the well. It was about noon.
>
> A Samaritan woman came to draw water, and Jesus said to her, "Give me a drink." (His

disciples had gone to the city to buy food.)
The Samaritan woman said to him, "How is it
that you, a Jew, ask a drink of me, a woman of
Samaria?" (Jews do not share things in common
with Samaritans.) Jesus answered her, "If you
knew the gift of God, and who it is that is saying
to you, 'Give me a drink,' you would have
asked him, and he would have given you living
water." The woman said to him, "Sir, you have
no bucket, and the well is deep. Where do you
get that living water? Are you greater than our
ancestor Jacob, who gave us the well, and with
his sons and his flocks drank from it?" Jesus said
to her, "Everyone who drinks of this water will
be thirsty again, but those who drink of the
water that I will give them will never be thirsty.
The water that I will give will become in them a
spring of water gushing up to eternal life." The
woman said to him, "Sir, give me this water,
so that I may never be thirsty or have to keep
coming here to draw water."

Jesus said to her, "Go, call your husband,
and come back." The woman answered him, "I
have no husband." Jesus said to her, "You are
right in saying, 'I have no husband'; for you
have had five husbands, and the one you have

now is not your husband. What you have said is true!" The woman said to him, "Sir, I see that you are a prophet. Our ancestors worshiped on this mountain, but you say that the place where people must worship is in Jerusalem." Jesus said to her, "Woman, believe me, the hour is coming when you will worship the Father neither on this mountain nor in Jerusalem. You worship what you do not know; we worship what we know, for salvation is from the Jews. But the hour is coming, and is now here, when the true worshipers will worship the Father in spirit and truth, for the Father seeks such as these to worship him. God is spirit, and those who worship him must worship in spirit and truth." The woman said to him, "I know that Messiah is coming (who is called Christ). When he comes, he will proclaim all things to us." Jesus said to her, "I am he, the one who is speaking to you."

Just then his disciples came. They were astonished that he was speaking with a woman, but no one said, "What do you want?" or, "Why are you speaking with her?" Then the woman left her water jar and went back to the city. She said to the people, "Come and see a man who told me everything I have ever done! He cannot be the Messiah, can he?" They left the city and were on their way to him. . . .

Many Samaritans from that city believed in him because of the woman's testimony, "He told me everything I have ever done." So when the Samaritans came to him, they asked him to stay with them; and he stayed there two days. And many more believed because of his word. They said to the woman, "It is no longer because of what you said that we believe, for we have heard for ourselves, and we know that this is truly the Savior of the world" (Jn. 4:3–30; 39–42).

## Reflection Questions

1. This is an instance of Jesus's generous treatment, or portrayal of, someone from Samaria. Another is his making a Samaritan the hero of one of his parables: the "Good Samaritan" (Lk. 10:25–37). It's also an example of his speaking to a woman, which "astonished" the disciples. What do these actions say to you about Jesus's desire for reaching out? What do they say about God's desire to reach out to you?

2. Jesus is clear about his identity: "I am he," he says. In other words, the Messiah. But knowledge of Jesus came only after the Samaritan woman was open with him. What have you learned about God after you were honest about your sexuality or identity with other people, and with God?

3. Jesus needs something from the woman—a drink. What does God "need" from you? In other words, what might God be asking of you in your life?

4. The woman is carrying a heavy water jar, an image of her burdens. She also needs something from Jesus: "living water." What burdens would you like to set down next to Jesus? And what do you need from him? Can you ask him?

5. Do you think the woman sounds suspicious of Jesus? Or surprised? Have you ever doubted that God wants to encounter you? Why?

6. The woman shares her history honestly with Jesus. "I have no husband," she says. Do you feel comfortable sharing some of your history with God? Why not share it in prayer?

7. This is one of the longest dialogues that Jesus has with someone in the Gospels. It takes time to come

to know someone. How have you let God know you? And how has God become known to you?

8. The New Testament scholar Sandra Schneiders, IHM, suggests that the woman's leaving behind her water jar is similar to the First Disciples, who "left everything" at the Sea of Galilee to follow Jesus (Lk. 5:11). And her testimony has a great effect among the Samaritans. Thus, she too is an apostle—"someone sent." How does God's activity in your life encourage you to be "someone sent"? What would you proclaim?

9. *For families, friends, and allies:* The disciples are "astonished" that Jesus is speaking to a woman. (They were probably surprised he was speaking to a Samaritan too.) Have you ever known people who were surprised that your family member or friend was LGBT? How did it make you feel? What enabled Jesus to treat her with such care? What enabled him not to be bothered by what others thought? Can you speak to Jesus about your experiences? And can you let him speak to you about his?

# The Risen Christ
# Appears to Mary
# Magdalene

L ife often seems hopeless. In fact, after the Crucifixion, for the remainder of Good Friday and all of
Holy Saturday, the disciples were bereft. And fright-
ened. They wondered if the same fate that had befallen
their leader would happen to them. Their hope for the
world seemed to be gone. But the Resurrection shows
that life always triumphs over death, love always triumphs over hatred, and hope always triumphs over
despair.

In this Gospel, it was not to one of the "inner circle"—
that is, the twelve men—to whom the newly resurrected
Jesus appeared first, but to a woman. In the Gospel of

John, it is Mary Magdalene, not Peter, who is first tasked with announcing the Good News.

Indeed, for the space of time—minutes or hours—between when the Risen Christ appeared to her and when she announced the Resurrection to the disciples, Mary Magdalene *was* the church on Earth. To her alone was revealed the mystery of Jesus's life, death, and resurrection.

It's another reminder of God's love for those people often seen as "less than" by the rest of the world.

Early on the first day of the week, while it was still dark, Mary Magdalene came to the tomb and saw that the stone had been removed from the tomb. So she ran and went to Simon Peter and the other disciple, the one whom Jesus loved, and said to them, "They have taken the Lord out of the tomb, and we do not know where they have laid him." Then Peter and the other disciple set out and went toward the tomb. The two were running together, but the other disciple outran Peter and reached the tomb first. He bent down to look in and saw the linen wrappings lying there, but he did not go in. Then Simon Peter came, following him, and went into the tomb. He saw the linen wrappings lying there, and the cloth that had been on Jesus's head, not lying with the linen wrappings but rolled up in a place by itself. Then the other disciple, who reached the tomb first, also went in, and he saw and believed; for as yet they did not understand the scripture, that he must rise from the dead. Then the disciples returned to their homes.

But Mary stood weeping outside the tomb. As she wept, she bent over to look into the tomb; and she saw two angels in white, sitting where the body of Jesus had been lying, one at the head and the other at the feet. They said to her, "Woman, why are you weeping?" She said to them, "They have taken away my Lord, and I do not know where they have laid him." When she had said this, she turned around and saw Jesus standing there, but she did not know that it was Jesus. Jesus said to her, "Woman, why are you weeping? For whom are you looking?" Supposing him to be the gardener, she said to him, "Sir, if you have carried him away, tell me where you have laid him, and I will take him away." Jesus said to her, "Mary!" She turned and said to him in Hebrew, "Rabbouni!" (which means "Teacher"). Jesus said to her, "Do not hold on to me, because I have not yet ascended to the Father. But go to my brothers and say to them, 'I am ascending to my Father and your Father, to my God and your God.'" Mary Magdalene went and announced to the disciples, "I have seen the Lord"; and she told them that he had said these things to her (Jn. 20:1–18).

## Reflection Questions

1. Can you remember a time when life felt hopeless? What have been your Good Fridays and Holy Saturdays? What helped you to move ahead?

2. The Christian message centers on the Resurrection, which centers on hope. What gives you hope? What have been your "resurrections"?

3. Who gives you hope? Who announces the Good News to you? Who is your Mary Magdalene? And to whom do you announce the Good News?

4. For a time, as the Gospel of John depicts it, Mary Magdalene was the church on Earth. For to her alone had been revealed the "Paschal Mystery," that is, the life, death, and resurrection of Jesus. If

you had to name one person who was the church for you in a dark time, who would it be?

5. Can you thank God for the grace of being able to hope?

6. *For families, friends, and allies:* Where have you found signs of the Resurrection in the lives of your LGBT family members and friends? Where do you see it in the church?

# The Road to Emmaus

Often things seem hard to understand, and even harder to accept. That's the case for all of us at different points in our lives. The story of the two despairing disciples walking away from Jerusalem after the Crucifixion shows what happens when we allow God to open our eyes to a new way of seeing, when we allow ourselves to reflect on what God has been doing, and when we find God in the midst of community.

> Now on that same day two of them were going to a village called Emmaus, about seven miles from Jerusalem, and talking with each other about all these things that had happened. While they were talking and discussing, Jesus himself came near and went with them, but their eyes were kept from recognizing him. And he said

to them, "What are you discussing with each other while you walk along?" They stood still, looking sad. Then one of them, whose name was Cleopas, answered him, "Are you the only stranger in Jerusalem who does not know the things that have taken place there in these days?" He asked them, "What things?" They replied, "The things about Jesus of Nazareth, who was a prophet mighty in deed and word before God and all the people, and how our chief priests and leaders handed him over to be condemned to death and crucified him. But we had hoped that he was the one to redeem Israel. Yes, and besides all this, it is now the third day since these things took place. Moreover, some women of our group astounded us. They were at the tomb early this morning, and when they did not find his body there, they came back and told us that they had indeed seen a vision of angels who said that he was alive. Some of those who were with us went to the tomb and found it just as the women had said; but they did not see him." Then he said to them, "Oh, how foolish you are, and how slow of heart to believe all that the prophets have declared!

Was it not necessary that the Messiah should suffer these things and then enter into his glory?" Then, beginning with Moses and all the prophets, he interpreted to them the things about himself in all the scriptures.

As they came near the village to which they were going, he walked ahead as if he were going on. But they urged him strongly, saying, "Stay with us, because it is almost evening and the day is now nearly over." So he went in to stay with them. When he was at the table with them, he took bread, blessed and broke it, and gave it to them. Then their eyes were opened, and they recognized him; and he vanished from their sight. They said to each other, "Were not our hearts burning within us while he was talking to us on the road, while he was opening the scriptures to us?" That same hour they got up and returned to Jerusalem; and they found the eleven and their companions gathered together. They were saying, "The Lord has risen indeed, and he has appeared to Simon!" Then they told what had happened on the road, and how he had been made known to them in the breaking of the bread (Lk. 24:13–35).

## Reflection Questions

1. When were your eyes "kept from recognizing" God? What prevented you from seeing God in these moments?

2. One of my spiritual directors said that he considered "we had hoped" to be the saddest words in the Gospels. Was there ever a time when you despaired, like the two disciples on the way to Emmaus? How do you see that time now?

3. Some New Testament scholars have noted that the sex of the second disciple—the friend of Cleopas—is not mentioned. So the other disciple might have been his wife. Who has accompanied you in your times of despair? Who has walked by your side?

4. What enables you to notice the presence of God in difficult times?

5. If you told the story of your own "Road to Emmaus," what would that story be?

6. *For families, friends, and allies:* At various points in your life, your eyes may also have been "kept from recognizing" the presence of God's grace in the life of your family member or friend. What opened your eyes?

# A Prayer for When I Feel Rejected

The rash of suicides among LGBT youths cannot fail to move the Christian heart, or indeed any heart capable of compassion. Although every suicide is a terrible tragedy, the suicide of a young person who feels that his or her life will never change, and who moves toward despair as a result of bullying and harassment, seems especially poignant.

Many LGBT people, young and old, have told me how wounded they have felt by their churches and other religious organizations. Churches are invited to find a way to reach out more compassionately to LGBT youths, to help them feel valued and know that they are beloved by God—and by us. We must lead as Jesus did, first with welcome, not condemnation.

For my part, here is a prayer composed for all who feel excluded, rejected, marginalized, shamed, or persecuted, in any way or in any place, religious or otherwise.

# A Prayer for When
# I Feel Rejected

*Loving God,*
*you made me who I am.*
*I praise you and I love you,*
*for I am wonderfully made,*
*in your own image.*
*But when people make fun of me,*
*I feel hurt and embarrassed and even ashamed.*
*So please, God,*
*help me remember my own goodness,*
*which lies in you.*
*Help me remember my dignity,*
*which you gave me when I was conceived.*
*Help me remember that I can live a life of love,*
*because you created my heart.*

*Be with me when people make me feel "less than,"*
*and help me to respond the way you would want me to,*
*with a love that respects the other but also respects me.*
*Help me find friends who love me for who I am.*
*Help me, most of all, to be a loving person.*

*And, God, help me remember that Jesus loves me.*
*For he too was seen as an outcast.*
*He too was misunderstood.*
*He too was beaten and spat upon.*
*Jesus understands me and loves me with a special love,*
*because of the way you made me.*

*And when I am feeling lonely,*
*help me remember that Jesus welcomed everyone as a*
*   friend.*
*Jesus reminded everyone that God loved them.*
*Jesus encouraged everyone to embrace their dignity,*
*even when others were blind to that dignity.*
*Jesus loved everyone with the love that you gave him.*
*And he loves me too.*

*One more thing, God:*
*Help me remember that nothing is impossible with you,*
*that you have a way of making things better,*
*that you can find a way of love for me,*

*even if I can't see it right now.*
*Help me remember all these things*
*in the heart you created,*
*loving God.*

*Amen.*

# Questions for Book Groups and Personal Reflection

This reading and discussion guide has been designed to accompany *Building a Bridge,* by James Martin, SJ, to help you and your community more deeply reflect on his invitation to the Catholic Church and the LGBT community to draw closer together. We hope that it enables you and your community to grasp more fully Father Martin's contribution to this important conversation.

# Introduction to the Revised and Expanded Edition

1. James Martin, SJ, says that he learned a great deal after the publication of the first edition of this book, including the fact that "ministry to LGBT Catholics is a ministry not just to LGBT people but, increasingly, to the entire church" (p. 3). What kind of outreach can the church do, to take one example, for families of LGBT Catholics?

2. Father Martin says that the onus for "bridge building" should fall on the institutional church rather than on LGBT Catholics, "because it is the institutional church that has made LGBT Catholics feel marginalized, not the other way around" (p. 4). Do you agree?

3. The book does not address questions of sexual relations between same-sex couples or the question of same-sex marriage because, as Father Martin explains, the institutional church and most LGBT Catholics are too far apart on the issue, and he wanted to focus on "areas of possible commonality." Moreover, he says, the book is focused on dialogue and prayer, rather than on questions

of sexual morality. What do you think about his decision to focus on these "areas of possible commonality"?

## *Why I'm Writing*

1. Father Martin writes, "The LGBT community is still invisible in many quarters of the church. . . . The work of the Gospel cannot be accomplished if one part of the church is essentially separated from any other part. Between the two groups—the LGBT community and the institutional church—a great chasm has formed, a separation for which a bridge needs to be built" (p. 15). How familiar are you with the "chasm" he describes? In your opinion, why does this divide exist today?

2. What would it mean for both the Catholic Church and the LGBT community to treat each other with "respect, compassion, and sensitivity," the three virtues outlined in the *Catechism of the Catholic Church*? (p. 17). What might have to change? What could remain the same?

3. "Many people see the church as contributing to division, as some Christian leaders and their con-

gregations mark off boundaries of 'us' and 'them.'
But the church works best when it embodies the
virtues of respect, compassion, and sensitivity"
(p. 19). What examples can you think of where
Christians mark off these boundaries? What examples can you think of where Christians refuse to
do so? What effect does each approach have?

4. "For most LGBT people, however, the process of
   understanding that they are loved by God as they
   are, and the process of finding their place in the
   church, remain difficult" (p. 21). Why is this so?
   Have you or a loved one ever experienced this?

## A Two-Way Bridge

1. Father Martin suggests that much of the tension
   between the Catholic Church in the United States
   and the LGBT Catholic community results from
   "a lack of communication and a good deal of mistrust between LGBT Catholics and the hierarchy"
   (p. 29). In response, he proposes building "a bridge
   between that community and the church" (p. 29).
   Why do you think he uses the image of a bridge
   here? What does he gain by doing so?

## The "First Lane": From the Church to LGBT Catholics

### RESPECT

1. Father Martin calls for "respect" from the institutional church to the LGBT community, writing, "First of all, *respect* means, at the very least, recognizing that the LGBT community *exists*, and extending to it the same recognition that any community desires and deserves because of its presence among us" (p. 32). In your experience, does the institutional church recognize that the LGBT community "exists"? Why does something that seems so simple mean so much?

2. Have you been positively influenced by the gifts of LGBT Catholics? (pp. 39–41). What have these gifts been? And how might you "honor" them, to use the language of St. Paul?

3. How do you show LGBT people "respect"?

### COMPASSION

1. "The first and most essential requirement is lis-

tening" (p. 52). Think about the LGBT people in your life. What would it mean to listen to them even more fully? What might you have to do differently? What might the institutional church have to do? Why do you think listening is "essential"?

2. Father Martin shares six stories of LGBT people and their families and friends, which he hopes will encourage us to listen (p. 53–56). Which of these stories spoke most powerfully to you?

3. "Catholic leaders regularly publish statements—as they should—defending the unborn, refugees and migrants, the poor, the homeless, the aged. . . . But where are statements specifically in support of our LGBT brothers, sisters, and siblings?" (p. 58). In your opinion, is this a double standard? Why do you think it exists?

4. Among the statistics shared about LGBT suicides and bullying, Father Martin notes that lesbian, gay, and bisexual youth are almost five times as likely to have attempted suicide as straight youths. Were you surprised by this figure? What does this say about outreach to LGBT youth as a "life issue"?

5. How do you show LGBT people "compassion"?

## SENSITIVITY

1. Father Martin writes, "You cannot understand the feelings of a community if you don't *know* the community" (p. 64). How might you increase your knowledge of the LGBT community? If you could do that, what might be the result? How might the Catholic Church do this? What might be the result?

2. "But for Jesus there was no 'other.' Jesus saw beyond categories; he met people where they were and accompanied them" (p. 67). What might Jesus's words and deeds, and how he treated the marginalized, teach the contemporary church about how to relate to the LGBT community? What might they teach you?

3. What Gospel stories might apply to the invitation to treat LGBT people with "respect, compassion, and sensitivity"? What Gospel passages might relate to outreach to those who feel marginalized?

4. Beyond "respect, compassion, and sensitivity," what other virtues does the church need to model when it reaches out to the LGBT community?

5. How do you show LGBT people "sensitivity"?

## The "Second Lane": From LGBT Catholics to the Church

### RESPECT

1. To the LGBT Catholic community, Father Martin suggests, "This is the moment to set aside the us-and-them mentality, for there is no us and them in the church" (p. 77). Have you ever considered yourself an "us"? Have you ever felt like a "them"? What might it look like for LGBT Catholics to heed this advice?

2. Father Martin calls LGBT Catholics to both "ecclesial" and "human" respect in its engagement with the institutional church (p. 79). How does he define both terms? Why are both needed?

3. Father Martin acknowledges that it might be very difficult for LGBT Catholics to think about treating the institutional church with "respect, compassion, and sensitivity" because of the exclusion that many in this group have felt. Even if it's difficult, do you think it's still important for members of a marginalized group to proceed in this way? Or would you call for another approach?

4. What is your response to the story of the father of the gay man who met with his local bishop (pp. 81–85)? Did it leave you hopeful, despairing, or somewhere in between? Could this be a model for dialogue in the future?

## COMPASSION

1. Father Martin lists the many duties of bishops on pages 88–89. How many people, including members of the LGBT community, do you think are aware of those duties? How might being aware of those duties increase this community's compassion for those in the church who work as bishops?

2. Speaking from his own experience, Father Martin notes, "One gay friend of mine said that he was particularly angry in the wake of the clergy sex-abuse crisis. After years of trying to stay with the church, despite feeling unwelcome, he felt deeply betrayed by the institution. 'I was furious,' he told me. How could he accept condemnations of his own sexuality from members of the hierarchy who had covered up the crimes of sex abuse?" (p. 92). In the face of such situations, how can the LGBT community acknowledge the issues that it has with

the church without letting those issues prevent the building of the "two-way bridge" Father Martin calls for?

3. Is it possible to have compassion for a group or an individual that has marginalized you? How does this relate to Jesus's call to "love your enemies and pray for those who persecute you." (Matt 5:44)?

## SENSITIVITY

1. "We need to be sensitive to the fact that when Vatican officials speak—whether it is the pope or a Vatican congregation—they are speaking to the entire world, not just the West and certainly not just the United States" (p. 101). In other words, when we hear a pronouncement from the pope, for example, we are called to remember that he is speaking to Catholics worldwide. How does that aspect of the "universality" of the church influence your view of Catholicism?

2. Father Martin mentions the important role of prophecy in the church. Why do you think he does this? Where have you seen the church act prophetically on various issues? How is prophecy relevant to helping the LGBT community grow in

its sensitivity toward the church?

3. Richard Rohr, the Franciscan priest and author, has written that prophets "cannot be fully insiders, but they cannot throw rocks from outside either" (p. 103). How does this relate to the need to advocate for the LGBT community within the church?

## Together on the Bridge

1. Father Martin reminds both "groups": "Neither lane on that bridge is smooth. On this bridge, as in life, there are tolls. It costs when you live a life of respect, compassion, and sensitivity" (p. 104). What might living in this way "cost" members of the LGBT community? Members of the institutional church? What is at stake? What are you willing to "pay" in terms of "tolls"?

2. To the LGBT community, Father Martin asks, "What keeps the bridge standing? What keeps it from collapsing onto the sharp rocks? What keeps us from plunging into the treacherous waters below? The answer is: the Holy Spirit" (p. 108). How does the Spirit support us individually and as a community? What is the role of the Spirit in

building unity between these two groups? Do you believe that all are welcome in God's church?

## Biblical Passages for Reflection and Meditation

1. Which of these biblical passages spoke most to you? Why?

2. Which of these passages most surprised you? Was there one that challenged you to see the LGBT person or the institutional church in a new way? How?

3. In published interviews, Father Martin has noted that many reviewers have ignored this section of the book—the invitation to prayer. Why do you think this is so? Do you think people are, in general, more comfortable with dialogue than with prayer?

4. What other passages from the Old and New Testaments speak to you about God's outreach to the marginalized?

5. How would you describe Jesus's approach to those on the margins of society in his day? What does this say about your outreach and the church's outreach?

## A Prayer for When I Feel Rejected

1. Were you able to pray this prayer? What happened when you did?

2. What does it mean for all of us to be "wonderfully made"?

3. If you wrote a prayer for someone who felt rejected, what would you write?

## Final Questions

1. How has *Building a Bridge* challenged you? How has it consoled you? How has it changed the way that you think?

2. "Respect, compassion, and sensitivity," the three virtues from the *Catechism of the Catholic Church,* were mentioned often throughout this book. In which of these virtues do you think you are doing well? In which might you need to grow? Think about your answers specifically in terms of how you may more fully care for either the LGBT community or the church.

3. What virtues and actions, beyond what Father Martin suggests, might be needed to help build this bridge?

4. With whom might you need to have a conversation—to listen to, to ask questions of—in order to move forward in building this bridge?

5. Where do you see signs of the Holy Spirit at work in the church's outreach to the LGBT community?

6. How is the Holy Spirit moving you?

# ACKNOWLEDGMENTS

Many people contributed to the writing of this book, and I am grateful to them.

First, I would like to thank New Ways Ministry for inviting me to deliver the lecture upon which the first half of this book is based, especially Sister Jeannine Gramick, SL, and Francis DeBernardo. I would like to thank the Very Rev. John Cecero, SJ, and the Very Rev. Robert Hussey, SJ, the Jesuit Provincials of the USA Northeast and Maryland Provinces of the Society of Jesus, respectively, and Matt Malone, SJ, president and editor-in-chief of America Media, for their support of the original address and this book. Thanks also to Father Cecero, my Jesuit Provincial, for his formal ecclesiastical approval of the book as well.

Thanks also to my Jesuit brothers who have supported me in my informal ministry to the LGBT community over these many years. I am far from the only Jesuit who engages in this kind of ministry. I am also grateful to all my brothers who supported me in the publication of this book, in so many beautiful ways.

Thanks to the pioneers in this ministry, like Sister Jeannine, her New Ways Ministry cofounder the Rev. Robert Nugent, and John McNeill, a former Jesuit priest and author of *The Church and the Homosexual*, a controversial book that was nonetheless published with ecclesial approval in 1976. Father Nugent died in 2014; Mr. McNeill in 2015. All three suffered in different ways as a result of their ministries.

Also, I would like to thank the Rev. Msgr. John Strynkowski; James Alison; William A. Barry, SJ; James F. Keenan, SJ; Michael O'Loughlin; Arthur Fitzmaurice; Xorje Olivares; and Dan De Brakeleer for their comments on both the talk and the manuscript. Thanks to Joseph McAuley at *America* and Heidi Hill for their careful fact-checking. Thanks to Mickey Maudlin, Mark Tauber, Anna Paustenbach, Noël Chrisman, Ann Moru, Mary Grangeia, Dianna Stirpe, Melinda Mullin, and Adia Colar of HarperOne for their careful edits, suggestions, and support of this book. Thanks to Donald Cutler for being such a wonderfully supportive literary agent. Thanks to Adrian Morgan for an eye-catching cover. And I would like to thank Ivan and Marcos Uberti for their friendship and support.

Most of all, I want to thank the many LGBT Catholics who have shared their experiences of the ways God has been at work in their lives. They have shown me what it means to be "wonderfully made."